"*Beyond Accompaniment* offers a solid combination of sound theology, a good grasp of the principles of conflict transformation, and a strong vision of renewed community that will serve as a model for parishes and other organizations trying to work their way beyond past wounds to a revitalized communion. The clear, step-by-step presentation William Nordenbrock provides can help guide troubled and conflicted communities to a deeper appreciation of their own hidden gifts and to an imaginative revisioning of their future. Highly recommended for any parish or church organization wanting to move themselves forward in greater faithfulness and discipleship."

— Robert Schreiter
Author of *The Ministry of Reconciliation*

"Thorough, precise, well researched . . . the elegance of the simplicity of his writing style just jumps off the pages. . . . [Nordenbrock's] concise explanation of [Appreciative Inquiry] and his masterful implementation of it is textbook perfect in my opinion. In truth anyone trying to understand and then use [this] process would do well to immerse her/himself in *Beyond Accompaniment*."

— Ralph Bonaccorsi
Office of Conciliation
Chicago, Illinois

Beyond Accompaniment

Guiding a Fractured Community to Wholeness

William A. Nordenbrock, CPPS

LITURGICAL PRESS

Collegeville, Minnesota

www.litpress.org

Cover design by Ann Blattner.
Photos: Congregation image by Gene Plaisted, OSC, © The Crosiers.
Church steeple image, Photos.com.

Excerpts from David Cooperrider and others, *Appreciative Inquiry Handbook: The First in a Series of AI Workbooks for Leaders of Change*, 2nd ed. Brunswick, OH: Crown Custom Publishing, Inc., 2005. Used by permission.

Excerpts from "The Distinctive Characteristics of Christian Reconciliation," an unpublished paper by Robert J. Schreiter, used by permission.

"Prayer to Consecrate Sacred Space" by Joseph Nassal, CPPS, used by permission.

Scripture texts in this work are taken from the New Revised Standard Version Bible © 1989, Division of Christian Education of the National Council of the Churches of Christ in the United States of America. Used by permission. All rights reserved.

1   2   3   4   5   6   7   8   9

Library of Congress Cataloging-in-Publication Data

Nordenbrock, William A.
    Beyond accompaniment : guiding a fractured community to wholeness / William A. Nordenbrock.
        p.   cm.
    Includes bibliographical references and index.
    ISBN 978-0-8146-3307-6 — ISBN 978-0-8146-3938-2 (e-book)
        1. Church controversies—Catholic Church.   2. Reconciliation—Religious aspects—Catholic Church.   3. St. Agatha Catholic Church (Chicago, Ill.)—Case studies.   I. Title.

BX1795.C69N67 2010
253—dc22

                                                            2010030854

Contents

List of Appendixes   vii

Introduction   ix

Section One

Chapter 1   A Church of Communion   3

Chapter 2   Toward a Practical Theology of Reconciliation   16

Chapter 3   Appreciative Inquiry: Theory and Process   40

Section Two

Chapter 4   A Community's Journey of Reconciliation:
Walking in Faith and Moving Forward
with Christ   65

Chapter 5   Discovery: How Has God Blessed
St. Agatha Church?   84

Chapter 6   Dream: St. Agatha's Faithful Future   97

Chapter 7   Design and Doing It: How Will St. Agatha Live
the Dream into Reality?   109

Section Three

Chapter 8   Restoring Communion through Appreciative
Inquiry   121

Chapter 9   Reconciliation and Communion Ecclesiology at
St. Agatha Church   129

Conclusion   The Place of Appreciative Inquiry in the
Praxis of Reconciliation   143

Epilogue   153

Appendixes   156

Notes   192

Bibliography   202

Index   205

Appendixes

Appendix A   The DNA of Appreciative Inquiry   156

Appendix B   Appreciative Inquiry 4-D Cycle   157

Appendix C   Appreciative Discernment 4-D Cycle   158

Appendix D   St. Agatha Parish Leadership Meeting:
              Outline   159

Appendix E   St. Agatha Leadership Meeting:
              Interview Guide   162

Appendix F   Discovery Phase Interview Guide   164

Appendix G   Interview Summary Sheet   168

Appendix H   Outline for Session One: Discovery   170

Appendix I   Session One: Small-Group Leader's Guide   172

Appendix J   Prayer to Consecrate Sacred Space   174

Appendix K   St. Agatha's Positive Core   175

Appendix L   Session Two: Small-Group Leader's Guide   177

Appendix M   Outline for Session Two: Dream   180

Appendix N   The Dream of St. Agatha Catholic Church   182

Appendix O   Six Possibility Propositions   183

Appendix P   Outline for Session Three:
Design and Doing It   185

Appendix Q   Possibility Proposition:
Be Church after Church   188

Appendix R   Action Plan: Be Church after Church   190

Introduction

In Roman Catholic circles today, to speak about the "polarized church" has almost become a redundancy; is there any other kind of church? It is seemingly impossible to gather in a group of Catholic ministers without the conversation becoming a telling of "war stories." No matter the ministry setting of the participants—education, parochial, religious congregational leadership, or other—often the topic becomes the difficulty of ministering within a church that is fragmented along ideological and theological lines. The stories will seldom speak of the value or gift of diversity within the affected faith community, because the diversity seems to be inseparably linked to a righteous and vocal intolerance. Usually in these discussions, it becomes quite apparent, although not frequently acknowledged, that the complaining ministers often speak out of their own ideological mindset and are not innocent bystanders to the conflicts and fragmentation that is their source of concern.

In his book, *A People Adrift: The Crisis of the Roman Catholic Church in America*, Peter Steinfels places the contentious and fragmented culture that is visible in the Catholic Church within the broader context of society. Noting the size of the church in relation to the population of the United States (roughly one fourth of the population), he sees it as inevitable that, as a sub-culture within the whole, the church would be influenced by our national ethos. He writes:

A church that embraces so many different groups inevitably becomes not only a bridge but also the battleground for the culture wars dividing American society. Many of the issues facing Catholicism mirror those of the larger society: anxiety over rapid change, sexuality, gender roles, the family; a heightening of individualism and distrust of institutions; the tension between inclusiveness and a need for boundaries; a groping for spiritual meaning and identity; doubts about the quality of leadership.[1]

While his observation resonates with a certain obviousness, it raises an important question as to our understanding of the church and the appropriate relationship of the church to the world. Who should be influencing whom?

The conflicts present within the church are not limited to ideological or theological differences. Especially at the level where people live, their local faith community, we sometimes appear to be a large family squabbling. I've heard stories of squabbles about liturgical practice, about the exercise of authority and how decisions get made, about conflicts that arise out of personality clashes between staff or church members, and many other stories of faith communities that have fractured relationships because of conflict.

Another source of a fracturing of the community is the misdeeds of clergy or other leaders of the faith community. There are many well-publicized stories of the life of the community being severely damaged by the betrayal of trust of a pastor that sexually abuses a child or the staff person who embezzles funds. As the horrendous accusations get made and the stories get told, the members of the faith community struggle to comprehend the new information and to reconcile it with their own experiences of the accused pastor who ministered to them when they were mourning or who helped them celebrate the important family faith moments of baptisms and weddings. The relationship of the faith community is distressed as some seek to support the accused and others reach out in compassion to those who report the abuse.

Still another category of conflict seems to be around the diffi-
culties that a faith community experiences when trying to create
community of those of different cultural backgrounds. These
cultural differences may be tied to ethnic differences that need
to be addressed as a result of immigration or migration patterns
within an urban area, but this is also the result of the declining
numbers of clergy and the perceived need to consolidate
parishes. These parishes may or may not have similar ethnic
heritages, but each parish has its own way of doing things and
relating to one another as a community of faith. Sometimes a
consolidation is like mixing water and oil.

So, how does a church leader respond to this fracturing of the
community? How can the pastoral exercise of leadership facilitate the healing of the community and the reconciliation that is
needed to restore the community into right relationship, to restore the communion of the faithful?

It is this pastoral concern that continues to grow within me.
I am a member of the Missionaries of the Precious Blood and
we claim reconciliation as an element of our charism. As a staff
member of the Precious Blood Ministry of Reconciliation (PBMR)
we are developing a ministry that responds to the need for reconciliation within the church. Simply, the church must respond
to this need for reconciliation within the church, and pastoral
leaders need to acquire the understanding and develop a pastoral approach to facilitate the healing of the Body of Christ.

It needs to be said that there can be no single pastoral approach
for promoting reconciliation within the church. A pastoral leader
who wishes to respond to conflict within the faith community
and be an agent of reconciliation needs a pastoral methodology
that has a broad range of methodological options, all of which
must be grounded in an authentic ecclesiology and an understanding of a Christian theology of reconciliation. In this book
I will explore one such approach, placing it within that theological framework.

Within the PBMR, a praxis for the ministry is developing using
the practical theology approach of: praxis, theological reflection,

praxis. The story that I will tell of my ministry with St. Agatha Catholic Church was my thesis project for a doctor of ministry degree. I approached the leadership of the parish with a simple proposal: let's see if we can develop a pastoral approach that will help this community experience healing and create a model that others can use as well. They responded and were as motivated by the desire to create something that can help others as they were by their own desire for healing.

What we discovered together is that a pastoral approach that is rooted in Appreciative Inquiry (AI) can be an effective strategy for promoting reconciliation and the restoration of communion in an ecclesial setting. AI is an organizational dynamics theory that is recent in its development, and it offers a radical shift in our understanding of organizations and organizational change theory. From my first exposure to the theory in the reading of James D. Ludema's article, "From Deficit Discourse to Vocabularies of Hope: The Power of Appreciation,"[2] I was intrigued by AI's potential to contribute to the praxis of reconciliation. Subsequent reading and course work excited me as I began to envision how the theory might be applicable in ecclesial settings and provide another "tool" that can be used in a ministry of reconciliation.

This book is written to share that tool with others and is done as an encouragement for those who see the need for reconciliation within their faith community and struggle to find a way to respond. When faced with the task of leading a fractured community, hope is often the first virtue to leak out of the cracks. Healing and reconciliation are possible. Effective pastoral response is possible.

I am a Roman Catholic priest and my writing will reflect that background and my denominational concern. While I acknowledge that orientation, the concern for reconciliation is not uniquely Catholic. It is my hope that this book will have applications beyond my denomination and will offer hope and guidance for ministry regardless of one's denominational commitment.

The book will unfold in three sections along the following trajectory. The first section is to provide the necessary foundation. Chapter 1 presents a vision of a church in communion. This communion ecclesiology is not an elaborate theological construction. Rather, it focuses on the spiritual underpinning of a faithful people who are in communion with God and one another. Chapter 2 offers a practical theology of reconciliation that brings together theological and sociological perspectives. Chapter 3 is given to the task of presenting a concise understanding of Appreciative Inquiry theory and process.

The middle section of the book tells in four chapters the story of the pastoral intervention at St. Agatha Catholic Church in Chicago. St. Agatha was a community that had suffered the betrayal of trust of a pastor who had abused young members of the school and parish. My work with them spanned over six months, as I assisted a new pastor and the parish leadership team to seek renewal and healing for their parish.

In the final section of the book, we reflect on the Appreciative Inquiry process at St. Agatha. First, we hear from the members of the parish leadership team as they reflect on the experience and its impact on their parish. Second, I offer my reflections on the process, specifically in light of the spiritual foundations found in communion ecclesiology and a Christian understanding of reconciliation. A final chapter offers the reader who shares a desire to effect reconciliation within the church some challenges and encouragements.

The book concludes with an epilogue written by Rev. Larry Dowling. Dowling was the pastor assigned to St. Agatha after the abuse was reported and the former pastor was removed. He figures prominently in the narrative that is told in the middle section of this book, and two years after the process he remains the pastor of St. Agatha. In the epilogue, he shares his current observations of the continuing effect of the AI process at St. Agatha. I am very grateful for his review and feedback of the middle section of this manuscript.

Along with my appreciation for Larry Dowling, I am especially grateful to the wonderful people of St. Agatha Catholic Church in Chicago. They were and continue to be a welcoming and hospitable community that inspires me with their sincere and Spirit-filled worship and their lived desire to faithfully walk with Christ. I will continue to use them as my example of a Catholic parish at its best! In particular, along with the pastor, the members of the core team for this project were thoughtful partners in this ministry of reconciliation, without whom this project would have been impossible. In the beginning, I expressed to them the desire that together we would create a model of responding to conflict and polarization present within the church. They are true cocreators of what you read in this book. May God's blessings continue to flow among them as they live their way into their dream.

Rev. Edward Foley, Capuchin, also contributed significantly to this work. He was my D. Min. thesis project director and it was through him that I was first exposed to the theory of Appreciative Inquiry. It was through his mentoring that I began to see the possible application of Appreciative Inquiry for the restoration of communion in fractured faith communities. During my ministry at St. Agatha he was a constant encouragement and a professional sounding board who helped to shape the project.

Finally, I want to acknowledge the role of my religious congregation, the Missionaries of the Precious Blood. We claim a ministry of reconciliation as an essential element of our charism, a self-understanding that is largely due to the work of Rev. Robert Schreiter, CPPS. It is his work that is at the heart of chapter 2. As our "family theologian" he has made accessible a theological framework for understanding reconciliation and helped to create a desire within our membership to live a spirituality of the reconciliation. I'm also deeply in debt to the many confreres who, through dialogue and shared expressions of our spirituality, helped to form my understanding and commitment to a ministry of reconciliation. Especially I wish to recognize those with whom I was privileged to create the Precious Blood Ministry of Reconciliation in Chicago. As we continue to work together in that ministry, we nurture the hope and dream that reconciliation is possible. Their accompaniment fuels my passion for reconciliation within our church.

I would be happy to receive your comments and questions on my work at St. Agatha and the role that Appreciative Inquiry can have in a ministry of reconciliation and other efforts at renewal within the church and faith communities. I can be engaged in dialogue through my e-mail account: bill.nordenbrock@gmail.com or contacted through the Precious Blood Ministry of Reconciliation in Chicago.

SECTION ONE

CHAPTER ONE

A Church of Communion

In the 2004 Catholic Common Ground Initiative lecture, the journalist John Allen noted that while there is much discussion within the church in regard to the polarization that is experienced, there is very little dialogue. He writes:

> When it comes time for discussion, I am often startled at how quickly things degenerate into disputation. The alarming phenomenon is not merely that Catholics seem angry with one another, but that they increasingly seem to be speaking separate languages. Self-identified "progressive" Catholics read their own publications, listen to their own speakers, attend their own conferences, and think their own thoughts. Self-identified "conservatives" do the same thing. Hence when you bring people from these two camps into the same room, they have moved so far down separate paths that even if there is good will for a conversation, quite often a shared intellectual and cultural framework is missing.[1]

It is with a hope for unity that Allen notes that the needed intellectual and cultural framework for the mutually respectful dialogue must be found in Catholic tradition.

The theologian and ecclesiologist Dennis Doyle looks to communion ecclesiology to provide that needed framework. "The problem facing U.S. Catholicism today lies not so much in its diversity," he writes, "as in the lack of a unifying vision that mediates among the various stances and approaches to provide some sense of a shared Catholic identity."[2] Doyle believes communion ecclesiology offers such a needed vision. He begins his work *Communion Ecclesiology* with the declaration, "The vision of the Church as communion enlightens and inspires. The process of dialogue in the spirit of communion fosters hope and encouragement."[3]

I approach communion ecclesiology from the pastoral concern of one who ministers within the church with a particular concern for reconciliation within that church. I experience the fragmentation and division within the church to be scandalous—in the strict sense that this very public polarization hinders the evangelical mission of the church. The church cannot effectively preach the Good News of Jesus unless we are a more visible embodiment of the Word that we preach. But the scandal is deeper than the hindering of the mission; it is an unfaithfulness to what the church is called to be. The French-Canadian theologian Jean-Marie Tillard puts it quite succinctly when he writes:

> It is very obvious that the Christian witness as such (the *martyria*) is tied to the visible unity of the disciples of Christ. Because how can one announce *truly* and in a credible way the Gospel of reconciliation in Jesus Christ while presenting oneself to the world as disciples of Christ who are divided among themselves and have put up new barriers? But what is at stake here is not limited to the missionary impact of the message. It is essentially a question of being what one is called to be, of doing what is necessary so that the work of God has the quality that it should have, to glorify the Father by manifesting the authentic nature of his plan, of giving Salvation its full dimension.[4]

I am far from unique in holding this concern. In those recurring discussions that I spoke of in the opening paragraph of the introduction, always the recognized need and desire for reconciliation is present in those groups of ministers telling the horror stories of a polarized church. We all desire and hope for a vision of church that we can present to our fellow believers, through preaching and lived witness, which can inspire others and promote the healing of the divisions that fracture our unity.

For Doyle "communion ecclesiology is a content and a process, a vision and a summons to higher ground."[5] Put another way, for one who seeks reconciliation within the church, communion ecclesiology is a vision that we strive to embody and it is a spirituality that we must live if we are to fulfill that vision.

The development of communion ecclesiology is dynamic and ongoing. Our current understanding has grown out of the interplay of many voices over time. In his book, Doyle draws on many theological sources to present an understanding of communion ecclesiology.

Among the various versions of communion ecclesiology, Doyle finds four elements that are seemingly always present. The first is that communion ecclesiology is an effort of *ressourcement*, that is, an attempt to connect with the original vision of the church held by the first millennium Christians, prior to the division among the Eastern Orthodox, Roman Catholic, and Protestant Christians. Second, communion ecclesiology places an emphasis on the spiritual relationship between humans and humans with God, over the more juridical and institutional aspect of the church. While there are multiple versions of communion ecclesiology, the foundational understanding is that the church is best understood in terms of relationships. The church is constituted by our relationship with God and one another. Third, communion ecclesiology holds the shared participation in Eucharist as being a needed visible sign of unity. And finally, there is a dynamic interplay between unity and diversity.[6]

Recognizing that there are many legitimate theologies of communion ecclesiology, Doyle presents a sort of synthesis and outlines a communion ecclesiology that seeks to bring together into a web of understanding five versions or dimensions: divine, mystical, sacramental, historical, and social. For Doyle, these five dimensions must be present within a communion ecclesiology that is faithfully "catholic." While Doyle looks for these elements in the various theological approaches that he explores in his book, it is the very influential French theologian Henri de Lubac that he cites as offering the best synthesis of these five dimensions.

Five Dimensions of Communion Ecclesiology

The Church Is Divine

An important and essential dimension of communion ecclesiology is that our understanding of our identity as a church is rooted in our belief in the doctrine of the Trinity. Henri de Lubac wrote, "God did not make us . . . for the fulfilling of a solitary destiny; on the contrary, He made us to be brought together into the heart of the life of the Trinity. . . . The people united by the unity of the Father and the Son and the Holy Spirit: that is the Church."[7]

This element of the communion ecclesiology is based in an anthropology that rejects the notion that the individual is the basic unit of human reality and posits instead a view that humans are essentially social. This reflects the relational reality of the three persons within the one God: that God is both one and a community. For humankind, individuality remains crucial, but not more essential than community. Just as the unity of the three persons of the Trinity is essential to our understanding of God, our interrelatedness as humankind is a necessary element of understanding humankind. In this way, the Trinity provides the relational foundation for understanding the church, and in the vision of communion ecclesiology, the church is to be a visible sign of that Trinitarian unity.[8]

The Church Is Mystical

Closely related to the divine element, our understanding of the church must include a mystical element. The mystical church is more than a mere human institution and it is more than the "fallible receiver of divine revelations."[9] The church is a mystery that is itself a revelation of God.

Images found in Scripture and that are prominent in the documents of the Second Vatican Council are the church as the Body of Christ and the doctrine on the communion of the saints. These images highlight the mystical and transcendent nature of the church. In communion ecclesiology, the church is understood as being more than an institution that is rooted in a particular time and place; rather, it transcends those limitations to describe a relationship among all the faithful through all time.

Doyle again turns to Henri de Lubac to illustrate this dimension. "De Lubac grasped well the mystical form of relationality in which images and symbols are used to express glimpses of the Church as mystery. . . . The Church is truly the mystical Body of Christ in that it represents the spiritual and social reunification of the unity of humankind. The Church is truly the Bride of Christ because it is so closely united with him. The Church is our mother because it brings Christians to birth within the Body of Christ."[10]

The Church Is Sacramental

An important theme in the document *Lumen Gentium* is that the church is a kind of sacrament. Doyle gives inspirational credit to Henri de Lubac for this understanding. He quotes de Lubac: "If Christ is the sacrament of God, the Church is for us the sacrament of Christ; she represents him, in the full and ancient meaning of the term, she really makes him present."[11] Like Christ who is both fully human and fully divine, as a sacrament of Christ, the church too shares that dual nature. As a sacrament, the church has both visible and invisible elements.

Doyle describes the significance of the sacramental nature of the church succinctly. "The Church consists of sacramental communities of Christians who love each other. . . . The Eucharist is the celebration *par excellence* through which the reality of the Church finds its fullest expression."[12] It is in the sacrament of Eucharist that members of the church are united to Christ. It is in that union with Christ that all the members of the body are brought into one communion as the Body of Christ, revealing that, like the Eucharist, the communion of the church has both horizontal and vertical dimensions. It is Eucharist that signifies and creates the intimate communion of all the faithful, that is, the church.

The Church Is Historical

While some may lean toward an idea of church that is too human, the opposite is also detrimental to a catholic communion ecclesiology. It is equally a distortion to think of the church only in divine, mystical, or sacramental terms. Here we see the necessity of including both vertical and horizontal dimensions in our understanding. The church is also an institution of fallible human beings that is situated in a context of time and place. A catholic vision of communion ecclesiology must be willing to recognize the truth that the church that is situated in history has at times failed to live the divine elements; we have developed, changed, and, at times, erred grievously.

Within this dimension a useful image is that of the church as the pilgrim people of God. Offering a needed balance to the Body of Christ imagery of the mystical and sacramental church, the pilgrim people represent the human side of the church reality. The church has grown and developed organically over time—starting with a relationship between Jesus and his followers—and through time and in real places is expressed as the relationship between people and between people and God.

The Church Is Social

This final dimension is inextricably linked to the historical dimension. The church is a society of Christian believers. It is not possible to think of Christian belief as an individual or private practice, an individual relationship with Christ. Rather, Christian belief must be understood to include the horizontal dimension of the gospel. As the pilgrim people of God journey through time, they do so together.

Doyle writes, "The sacraments have a social dimension because as means of salvation they are instruments of unity."[13] While Eucharist is a sign of our unity as a church, that unity does not stop with the walls of the church building. Those who are present for the celebration of Eucharist are sent out to continue the evangelical and reconciling mission of Jesus. This mission into the world must arise from our understanding of the church as a lived solidarity with others. The important image of the church that expresses this dimension is the church as a leaven in the world.

Within communion ecclesiology, the image of the church as leaven in the world has important implications. Primarily, it projects an "understanding of the church as a social body with a commitment to social justice and to global relationality. Christian solidarity is complemented by human solidarity."[14] Second, it "expresses a vision of the world, with all of its ambiguities and negativities, as the essentially good arena in which the lives of those who belong to the Church are lived out."[15]

These five versions or dimensions of communion ecclesiology need to be held together to create the needed synthesis and we do that through the use of analogies. It is an analogical imagination that allows us to speak of the church as the Body of Christ and to appreciate that there is something holy and divine, mystical and sacramental about being the church. At the same time, we are able to speak of the church as the people of God and the leaven in the world and recognize that as a church we are part of a long lineage of fallible human beings with an unfolding history and an ever-changing and very diverse social context in which we try to live out our faith. We are both: we are a church that gazes heavenward in our response to God and a church that looks to the side and sees that same God in the lives we share with other believers.

The use of analogies to point to the various aspects of communion ecclesiology allows those competing elements to be held together in one theological construct. An analogy does not claim to be an all-inclusive definition or description, but an image that points toward a truth. It is through the use of multiple analogies that a multifaceted theological truth can take shape. Again, an example can be seen in the writing of de Lubac who could speak of the church as a bride of Christ to highlight the unity that the church has with Christ *and* speak of the church as the harlot of Christ to acknowledge that a church of humans is sometime unfaithful to that unity with Christ.[16] While the two analogies are starkly antithetical, neither analogy denies the truth indicated by the other. Many images are needed to hold the truth of our identity as a church.

Spirituality of Communion

My concern is the implications of communion ecclesiology for the spiritual life of the church. Being church is a spiritual activity and within communion ecclesiology is an inherent spirituality. I define spirituality simply (nonacademically) as a set of beliefs and values that serve to orient a person as they examine and live their life, particularly their relationship with God and others. Here my guiding questions will be: How do we live our way into the vision of communion ecclesiology? In particular, what does this vision require of a member of the church in their relationship with others within the church?

In the Apostolic Letter *Novo Millennio Ineunte*, Pope John Paul II wrote that "To make the Church *the home and school of communion*: that is the great challenge facing us in the millennium which is now beginning, if we wish to be faithful to God's plan and respond to the world's deepest yearning."[17] He then asks the important question: "But what does this mean in practice?"[18] He answers the question by saying that before making practical plans, what is needed is to promote a "spirituality of communion."[19]

John Paul II outlines a spirituality of communion with four elements or characteristics. The first is that a spirituality of communion must be mystical in that it is primarily rooted in the heart's contemplation of the mystery of the Trinity dwelling in us. Second, the spirituality embodies a solidarity with our brothers and sisters whom we recognize and accept as being part of ourselves in the unity of the Mystical Body. In this solidarity we are able to share in the joys and the sorrows of their lives and live together in a deep and genuine friendship. Third, that solidarity implies that we hold others in a positive regard, recognizing the giftedness of each person, gifts that are not just given to them directly but also given to us through our relationship with them. Finally, a spirituality of communion must embody a hospitality that knows how to "make room" for our brothers and sisters. Without following this spiritual path, John Paul II warns that any external structures of communion will serve little purpose and will be "mechanisms without a soul."[20]

A praxis of communion must be built on the foundation of a radical commitment to unity within the church. As noted above, this is a "duty" of all Catholics, but it is a duty that needs to be embraced not out of a sense of obligation but out of love for the vision of communion ecclesiology. To be in union with brothers and sisters in the church is a requirement of faithfulness, but the fulfillment of the requirement is the joy of communion.

To be in communion as a church is a measure of our faithfulness, both individually and communally. Our faithfulness to God is intrinsically linked to our communion with one another in the church. This twofold direction of faithfulness, the horizontal and the vertical, is apparent in the Scriptures and in communion ecclesiology. Yet it is a constant temptation to separate the love of God from our love of neighbor, to separate communion with God from communion as a church. It is the remembering and embracing of that inseparable link that helps us to make the radical commitment to unity.

It is Eucharist that provides the central image for church in communion ecclesiology and it is table fellowship that must be at the center of a praxis of communion. A radical commitment to unity includes a commitment to stay at the communion table. This has a twofold effect.

First, through our participation in the celebration of Eucharist, we keep the central image of communion ecclesiology before us. It is in the celebration of Eucharist that the divine, mystical, and sacramental dimensions of communion ecclesiology are made real; that which is invisible is now made visible. In receiving the Body (and Blood) of Christ, we are reminded that we do so as the Body of Christ.

Second, Eucharist is a sacrament of reconciliation. At Eucharist we remember and give thanks for the reconciliation of humankind through Christ. But even more so, through the prayer and sacramental action, we ask that any breaks in our communion be healed so that our unity will be restored. When we look across the table at one from whom we are estranged, we are reminded that we are part of a mystical union that is greater than that which separates us. The table of Eucharist is to be a bridge of communion and reconciliation.

The seeming failure of Eucharist to, in fact, effect reconciliation within a divided church, is a particular source of sadness. More so when the polarization that divided the community is liturgical, that is, about how we gather around the table. Such a situation, more than any other, requires of us that radical commitment to table communion.

Communion through Dialogue

Dialogue is also a key activity in the living of a spirituality of communion. Talking together (or at one another) becomes dialogue when the spiritual discipline of listening is joined with the speaking of truth. In faith communities or situations with diverse theological viewpoints, it is dialogue that can help us to restore or maintain communion.

Listening is a spiritual discipline. It is spiritual in that the motivation to listen to another in a situation of conflict must be based in our living a commitment to unity. It is a discipline in that it is often not easy and it requires practice. Often, listening is not something that we desire to do; simply avoiding conversation with another when we know we have differing theological positions often seems an attractive alternative. Without a spiritual commitment to communion and the discipline to live that spirituality, dialogue will not happen.

Dialogue involves the speaking of truth. If you have suffered through polarized and conflicted discussions, your immediate question might be: Whose truth? The answer, of course, is that each person must speak what they believe the truth to be but speak their truth recognizing and respecting the principle of plurality, that is, acknowledge that there does exist legitimate diversity in a church of communion. In fact, there is no communion without that diversity. To live a spirituality of communion is to cherish and work for a unity that is broad enough to hold all legitimate diverse viewpoints; it is not to call for a uniformity to that which I perceive to be the truth.

In the Catholic Common Ground Initiative lecture previously cited, John Allen presented a spirituality of dialogue. It is offered here as a way to broaden the scope of discussion about the role of dialogue in the praxis of communion. That spirituality was presented through a schema containing five key elements.

"The first is a dose of epistemological humility."[21] By this Allen simply means that we need to be willing to admit that we do not know everything. Hence, we should be open to the possibility that others might have something to teach us. If we rush to form our own opinion, without the encounter with others through dialogue, we lose the opportunity to find the truth in that situation.

"The second is a solid formation in Catholic tradition as a means of creating a common language."[22] There can be no dialogue without a common language that arises out of a shared intellectual understanding. Allen illustrates this point by noting the difficulty that many Americans have in understanding the documents that come out of the Vatican. Because those statements are written with an assumption of classic Aristotelian-Thomistic cultural formation but are read by those with a liberal democratic worldview, the result is often confusion and anger. It takes much dialogue to "translate" meaning between intellectual frameworks and to establish a shared framework.

This highlights the need for the third element in a spirituality of dialogue, which is patience. Coming to a common understanding often requires that we dedicate the time needed to arrive at that understanding. "If the unity of the church is important [read: *if we have made a radical commitment to unity*], then we need to give time to those with whom we tussle, time to understand and to be challenged."[23]

"Fourth, a spirituality of dialogue requires perspective, meaning the capacity to see issues through the eyes of others."[24] In this, I hear an echo of the call of John Paul II to live a spirituality of communion in solidarity with our brothers and sisters, seeing them with a positive regard as a gift to the church.

"Fifth and finally, we must foster a spirituality of dialogue that does not come at the expense of a full-bodied expression of Catholic identity. There is no future for dialogue if convinced Catholics sense the price of admission is setting aside their convictions."[25] In *Novo Millennio Ineunte* John Paul II writes that "dialogue cannot be based on religious indifferentism" but must be rooted in the truth that we believe.[26] The context of his statement is interreligious dialogue and the missionary duty of the church for the proclamation of the Word, but it is equally applicable as a principle for a spirituality of dialogue within the church. He continues by saying that our "missionary duty does not prevent us from approaching dialogue *with an attitude of profound willingness to listen*" because of our belief in the presence of the mystery of grace that is the Holy Spirit.[27] In the same manner, dialogue in the church must permit the expression of the truth that the participant believes, but speakers of truth must also be guided by a spirituality of communion that opens them to the presence of the Spirit in the words of others.

With this fifth element of his spirituality of dialogue, Allen has perhaps identified the largest obstacle to dialogue between self-identified progressives and self-identified conservatives within the church. Among conservatives, "dialogue" has come to mean conceding to relativism at the expense of truth. With them, there can be no dialogue unless the groundwork is laid to create a place where they can safely express their convictions. This does not mean that conservatives should be excused from giving an honest hearing to others who hold convictions that are contrary to their own, but praxis must account for their suspicion of dialogue.

By way of conclusion, I return to the importance of analogies. Our ability to live a spirituality of communion and dialogue is fostered when we have an appreciation for analogies and develop our analogical imagination. When we are able to speak analogically, we are able to express the truth of our own convictions, and to leave room in the dialogue for the expression of convictions that we do not share. It is in making room for the other that communion is fostered. And it is in communion that we realize a vision of church that is faithful and expressive of our catholic tradition.

Tillard reminds us that "Communion is not the same as a gathering together of friends. . . . It is the coming together in Christ of men and women who have been reconciled."[28] For Tillard, the church is formed through reconciliation that leads to communion. He writes: "The Church in this world is nothing more than the concrete portion of humanity inscribed into the sphere of reconciliation opened up by the Cross. Viewed from a historical perspective it proves to be the work of the Spirit taking human tragedy and immersing it in the power of communion and the peace of the Cross so that . . . the design of the Father will come to fruition."[29]

While communion is the vision that can guide the church, it is the embodiment of a spirituality of communion that must be the visible sign of God's plan for the community of the faithful. The hallmark of that plan of God is that all are reconciled in Christ. It is to reconciliation that I now turn.

CHAPTER TWO

Toward a Practical Theology of Reconciliation

It is one thing to say that we desire reconciliation in the church, but precisely what do we mean by "reconciliation"? Reconciliation is a hot topic in the church these days. It was the primary consideration for the 2009 Synod for Africa. The Holy Father convened bishops, theologians, and others who explored the role of reconciliation in the African church. Succinctly, they identified reconciliation as a key focus for the mission of the church in Africa and recognized the need for the African church to itself be reconciled.

While reconciliation is a hot topic in theological circles, it is also a concept in the forefront of peacemaking efforts in social or political arenas. Here we need think no further than the Truth and Reconciliation Commission that sought to build a new society in postapartheid South Africa. To understand the concept of reconciliation, we need to be willing to draw from both theological and secular disciplines.

In this chapter I draw on both theological and sociological sources to present an understanding of reconciliation that can be a practical foundation for a ministry. I begin with some theological considerations on the centrality of reconciliation to an understanding of the Incarnation and of the mission that is the church. Second, I specifically address the concept and practice of reconciliation. In my ministry of reconciliation, I have relied on two authors to provide a framework for reflecting theologically and practically on my work, Robert Schreiter and John Paul Lederach. In this chapter, I am only able to provide a brief overview of certain aspects of their work, sharing both theory and praxis considerations. I conclude the chapter by observing some of the parallels and differences in the work of the two scholars and presenting a synthesis of their work.

Some Theological Considerations[1]

Central to my understanding of the significance of the Incarnation is that the mission of Jesus was to bring about reconciliation. The definitive articulation of this is found in Ephesians 1:3-10:

> Blessed be the God and Father of our Lord Jesus Christ, who has blessed us in Christ with every spiritual blessing in the heavenly places, just as he chose us in Christ before the foundation of the world to be holy and blameless before him in love. He destined us for adoption as his children through Jesus Christ, according to the good pleasure of his will, to the praise of his glorious grace that he freely bestowed on us in the Beloved. In him we have redemption through his blood, the forgiveness of our trespasses, according to the riches of his grace that he lavished on us. With all wisdom and insight he has made known to us the mystery of his will, according to his good pleasure that he set forth in Christ, as a plan for the fullness of time, to gather up all things in him, things in heaven and things on earth.

In this Pauline teaching, the role of Jesus in the timeless plan of God is revealed. Jesus, through the redemptive shedding of his blood on the cross, fulfills the desire of God that we may be returned to our place as God's children. The covenant is renewed and made eternal as we are gathered back into the grace of communion with God. This is foundational to a Christian understanding of salvation history and community.

It was for reconciliation that God came to us in the person of Jesus. Simply, the mission of Jesus can be understood to be one of reconciliation. First of all, through the death and resurrection of Jesus, the way is open to all humankind to return to right relationship or communion with God. Second, the mission of Jesus was also essentially about the reconciliation of all humankind. The preaching ministry of Jesus, which finds its apex in the Sermon on the Mount narrative, is a call to establish the reign of God, a reign in which justice is the hallmark of God's children living together in right relationship and peaceful communion.

This is the twofold dimension of the reconciliation mission of Jesus: our redemption and reconciliation with God, won for us by Christ, is inseparable from the reconciliation and communion that Christians are to live with one another. Like the twofold commandment of love found in Luke 10:27 ("You shall love the Lord your God with all your heart, and with all your soul, and with all your strength, and with all your mind; and your neighbor as yourself"), reconciliation has both "vertical" and "horizontal" dimensions. They are two parts of the same reconciling work of Christ. "Vertical reconciliation is the reconciliation God works so as to restore humankind to communion with God. Horizontal reconciliation draws upon vertical reconciliation in order to bring about healing in human relations, either between individuals or between groups of human beings."[2]

The mission of the church is to continue that reconciling mission of Christ. The foundational passage for this is found in 2 Corinthians 5:17-20:

> So if anyone is in Christ, there is a new creation: everything old has passed away; see, everything has become new! All this is from God, who reconciled us to himself through Christ, and has given us the ministry of reconciliation; that is, in Christ God was reconciling the world to himself, not counting their trespasses against them, and entrusting the message of

> reconciliation to us. So we are ambassadors for Christ, since God is making his appeal through us; we entreat you on behalf of Christ, be reconciled to God.

All ministry in the church must be situated within this Christological understanding. As the continuation of the mission of Jesus, the faithfulness of the church must be examined in light of our ministry of reconciliation. Does the work of the church continue the twofold path of mediating the grace that brings about the reconciliation of sinners with God as well as mediating the grace that will bring to fruition the vision of the reign of God that will be recognized in the lived experience of the communion of the faithful? It is our answer to this question that largely provides the measure of our faithfulness in mission.

Theological Framework:
A Christian Spirituality of Reconciliation

Robert Schreiter is a Catholic priest and theologian who teaches at Catholic Theological Union in Chicago. Not only has he written and lectured extensively about reconciliation, but he is also actively engaged in applying the principles that he has developed in situations of conflict around the globe. In his writings, Schreiter presents an extensive framework for understanding a Christian ministry of reconciliation, which he articulates around five central points or characteristics.

1) *It Is God Who Initiates and Brings about Reconciliation*[3]

Reconciliation is, first and foremost, the work of God. Any ministry of reconciliation must "underscore Paul's insight that we participate in the ministry of reconciliation as ambassadors on behalf of Christ. . . . We participate in God's reconciling work."[4] This is an acknowledgment that the grace required to transform that which separates and divides the Christian community must have God as its source. "For that reason, it can be said that for the Christian reconciliation is more a spirituality than a strategy."[5] This does not mean that strategies are not part of a ministry of reconciliation. Strategies must be used to engage the parties in need of reconciliation. Rather, it acknowledges that a Christian praxis of reconciliation must be concerned with both the "vertical" and "horizontal" dimensions, for we are dependent on the gratuity of God.

Schreiter highlights two important implications of this characteristic of reconciliation. The first is that we must acknowledge that even the seemingly small offenses that separate two people can have implications that go beyond the human capability to heal. This is even more evident in large-scale social conflict. This recognition encourages one not to trivialize the damage that the wrongdoing inflicts. Second, when we participate in a ministry of reconciliation, we do so, as Paul says, as ambassadors acting on behalf of Christ (2 Cor 5:20). Because we are participating in the ministry of Christ, not our own, it underscores the importance for ministers of reconciliation to be grounded in a personal spirituality that allows them to listen to the inner voice of God and to allow themselves to be led by God's Spirit.[6]

2) *In Reconciliation, God Begins with the Victim*

God initiates this work of reconciliation in the lives of the victims. This is contrary to a common cultural understanding of reconciliation, at least in the United States. Typically, one might think of reconciliation as beginning with the wrongdoer coming to acknowledgment of their guilt and going to their victim to seek forgiveness. But Schreiter writes, "God begins with the victim, restoring to the victim the humanity which the wrongdoer has tried to wrest away or to destroy. This restoration might be considered the very heart of reconciliation."[7]

In his earlier work on reconciliation Schreiter spoke of the violence that is the cause of conflict as being a narrative of the lie. The stories that we tell about ourselves, our origins, and our important relationships (family, community, country) strongly shape our identity. Our identities are contained in the narratives that we tell of our lives.[8] "Violence tries to destroy the narratives that sustain people's identities and substitute narratives of its own. These might be called narratives of the lie, precisely because they are intended to negate the truth of people's own narrative."[9] In God's work of reconciliation, God begins with the victim as a way of bringing about the healing that can restore the truth of an individual's humanity, as told in the creation narratives, that all humankind is a mirror image of the divinity of the Creator.

Further support for this characteristic is found through reflection on the mission of reconciliation of Christ as told in the narrative of his death and resurrection. It is God who initiates this act of reconciliation. Christ, who is the ultimate victim, came not in response to the repentance of a sinful people, but as a gracious gift of mercy bestowed on the undeserving.

3) *In Reconciliation, God Makes of Both Victim and Wrongdoer a "New Creation" (2 Cor 5:17)*

While it is possible to think about reconciliation in terms of the restoration of right relationship, it is not a return of the relationship to its former state. Rather, something new is created. When there has been significant fracturing of the trust that is essential in relationships, there is no way to "forgive and forget"; there is no way to move into the future without the memory of the wrong that has been committed. Those events become a part of our identity as they reside in our memory. As Schreiter writes, however, "What happens in the healing that takes place in reconciliation is that we are taken to a new place, a place that we had not expected or measured out for ourselves. The moment of reconciliation comes, therefore, as a surprise, providing for us something that we could not have imagined."[10]

So while the memory of the past is retained, with reconciliation the memory is resituated within the context of the victim's life and it loses some of the toxicity or the power that it has to be the primary memory that determines the identity of the victim.

Perhaps the most significant aspect of this resituation of the memory is that the victim is sometimes able to forgive their wrongdoer. The great beneficiary of an act of forgiveness is the one who forgives and who in the act of forgiving may be liberated from the toxic power of the wrong done to them and is no longer hostage to it. They can now create a future that is not determined by the narrative of the lie, or the wrong done to them.[11]

In that act of forgiveness the wrongdoer is also made new because their identity is no longer defined by the wrong that they have committed. Rather, through the compassion of forgiveness, they are now seen as more than one who is defined by their misdeed, and they too can be created anew and be restored to a fuller humanity.

4) *Christians Pattern Their Suffering on the Suffering, Death, and Resurrection of Christ*

"For Christians, the 'master narrative' of divine reconciliation is found in the story of Christ's suffering, death, and resurrection."[12] For the Christian who has experienced trauma at the hand of another or the community that has been fractured by violence or wrongdoing, it is in that paschal mystery that we look for meaning.

While the Catholic tradition holds that suffering can be redemptive, the personal experience of suffering is often a shattering and faith-threatening experience. As a Christian seeks to discover meaning in the suffering that they have endured, often a first response is to believe that through their suffering God is revealing some larger purpose. Schreiter points out the danger of such thinking, which "may be guided by an oversimplified and even erroneous image of God as One who desires punishment or demands retribution."[13] An alternative, he continues, is for the one who has suffered to identify with Christ, who also suffered (unjustly) on the cross. "Because Christians believe that Jesus did undergo suffering and a terrible death, and that God did not allow him to remain in death, but raised him from the dead, identifying their own suffering with the suffering of the innocent Jesus becomes a way of surviving the depredations that suffering brings upon us."[14] A key element of this understanding is that in identifying with the Christ who suffers, the victim does not deny their suffering or minimize its impact on their life, but is able to be accompanied by Jesus through the suffering to reconciliation.

For those engaged in a ministry of reconciliation, the task is to accompany the one who suffers and to help them to find the means to recover their damaged humanity. To walk with another as they seek to pattern their life and the suffering that they have endured after the pattern of the cross and resurrection of Christ requires that the minister have the spiritual resources for the task.[15]

5) *Reconciliation Will Be Complete Only When God Has Reconciled the Whole World in Christ*

Anyone who has been engaged in the work of reconciliation knows the enormity of the mission and the difficulty of effectively constructing peace. While this is apparent when we look at the need for reconciliation in places of global conflict, it is equally true in our efforts to bring reconciliation in a family or church, or even between two individuals. Efforts at bringing about reconciliation often result in less than the desired outcome. So how does the minister of reconciliation maintain hope and motivations for the mission?

There are two beliefs that must be incorporated into the thinking of the minister. The first is to remember that reconciliation is both a goal and a process. Here the temptation is to lose sight of the process aspect in our desire to see the fulfillment of the goal of reconciliation. It is necessary to remember that God is the primary agent of reconciliation and it is God's work in which we participate. While some movement toward reconciliation is possible, it is often incomplete and it is not within our power to provide the healing that leads to forgiveness and reconciliation. We cooperate with God. This brings us to the second belief, which is articulated by St. Paul: "He has made known to us the mystery of his will, according to his good pleasure that he set forth in Christ, as a plan for the fullness of time, to gather all things in him, things in heaven and things on earth" (Eph 1:9-10).

The fullness of reconciliation will not be achieved until the end of time. On one level, this can be discouraging in the denial of the results we desire in the present time. For the Christian, however, it can also be a source of hope, a hope that arises out of a trust in the word and power of God. For a Christian, hope is sustained, not by the achievement of success, but by faith that God remains present and with us in those times when success is fleeting. That eschatological good news is a distinctive characteristic of a spirituality of reconciliation.

Contribution to Praxis

In his development of a theological framework for understanding a Christian spirituality of reconciliation, Schreiter has provided a foundation for a Christian ministry of reconciliation. From the theological base, he writes of the praxis of reconciliation, although he paints a picture with broad brush strokes.

An important source for Schreiter in this regard is the postresurrection appearance stories found in the gospels, which he reads with a hermeneutic of reconciliation. From these, he first identifies a pattern in the reconciliation ministry of Jesus, and from that he extrapolates to offer some implications for the praxis of reconciliation.

One such example is found in his reading of the breakfast at the seashore passage found in John 21:1-17. The story is familiar. Simon Peter and some of the others had returned to Galilee and had taken up their former way of life. It is as if, Schreiter suggests, they are wanting to close the book on the Jesus story.[16] It isn't going so well. They have fished all night without success.

Jesus enters the scene as an unrecognized stranger. He alters their fishing strategy and they are successful. In their success, they recognize Jesus and they return to shore, led by Simon Peter. The disciples not only are surprised to see that it is Jesus but also must be surprised to discover that he is cooking a meal for them. Schreiter observes that in this action Jesus combines table fellowship with hospitality.[17] Not only does Jesus cook for them, but he serves them that which is familiar to fishermen: fish. He also allows them to contribute to the meal from their work, affirming their value and contribution.

In this first part of the story, Schreiter identifies the first two steps in a methodology of a ministry of reconciliation being used by Jesus. The first step is the *accompanying* of victims and the second is the *providing of hospitality*. The accompaniment is seen in the initiative of Jesus to go to the disciples whose lives had been tossed into chaos by the event of his death and their failure, as yet, to grasp the significance of the resurrection. He listens to them and, as it were, meets them where they are. Hospitality is seen in that Jesus has found a way to make this encounter a safe place for the disciples, especially for Simon Peter, who had denied him. This is an important moment in a ministry of reconciliation because it creates "the atmosphere of trust which makes human communication possible again."[18]

The narrative continues with Jesus engaging Simon Peter in conversation; there is Jesus' threefold questioning of Peter's love for him and Peter's affirmation. Jesus' surprising response to Peter's answers is to instruct Peter to "feed my lambs." It is in this remarkable exchange that Schreiter identifies the remaining two steps in Jesus' method of ministry: *reconnecting* Peter to himself (Jesus) and to the community, and the *commissioning* of Simon Peter.

In giving Simon Peter the opportunity to affirm his love for Jesus, Jesus gave him a chance to express his sorrow and counter the threefold denial that was Peter's shameful part in the passion narrative of Jesus. In accepting the love of Peter, the love of Jesus for him was reaffirmed and their relationship was restored. And in the command to "Feed my sheep," Simon Peter is returned to right relationship with the community of the faithful as he is restored to his role as shepherd of the flock of Christ.[19]

To briefly summarize, we see in this ritual of a dialogue and the sharing of a meal, an act of reconciliation that restores communion. Again, this communion gets configured along the vertical and horizontal relationships—between Simon Peter and the risen Lord; and between Simon Peter and his fellow believers in the community of the faithful.

In his comments on this ministry of Jesus, Schreiter observes that the first two steps, accompaniment and hospitality, are places where the Christian community can be proactive in their ministerial response to conflict and the promotion of reconciliation. He writes: "Learning how to accompany, and learning how to create through hospitality an environment of trust, kindness and safety are disciplines that can be studied, practiced and learned."[20]

It is interesting to note that for Schreiter, this is more than the skill development of an individual, rather it is part of the creation of communities of reconciliation, which becomes the locus of the ministry of reconciliation. He says that these communities of reconciliation have three important and related aspects.[21]

The first is that they are communities of safety. Those who have been victimized need to have a safe place where they are able to explore their wounds. As a place of safety, the reconciling community is the antithesis of the place of violence. For the victim this safety is a necessary condition for the restoration of trust and is a sign that the violence they have experienced has ended and will not resume.

Second, communities of reconciliation are communities of memory. Here memories can be recovered and the possibility is presented that those memories may be understood within the framework of the paschal mystery. In situations where the need is for social reconciliation, the community of reconciliation can be a safe place where the people can come to arrive at a common memory of the past. "Communities of memory are also places where we learn again to speak the truth."[22] The telling of truth is necessary for the narrative of the lie to be refuted and for the people to retell the true narratives that reclaim their identity.

And finally, communities of reconciliation need to be communities of hope. It is here that the victims of violence can move beyond the day-to-day survival and come to experience a culture of hope where a future can be envisioned. "As with communities of memory, communities of hope work to build a common future in which all are safe, justice is done, and the truth is told."[23]

While the initial two phases in the reconciliation ministry of Jesus can be achieved through human endeavor, Schreiter clearly asserts that the latter two, the reconnection and the commissioning, reside solely in the action of God.[24] For many, the experience of reconciliation and healing happens upon the person as an unexpected event, an outpouring of divine benevolence and grace. Schreiter writes: "As ministers of reconciliation we can only mediate in indirect ways those connections and commissions; we do not create them. The spirituality needed for reconciliation is best developed in that learning to wait and listen that marks good accompaniment. We may end up helping the restored victims identify connections and commissions, but we are not their source."[25]

A Sociological Framework: Reconciliation and Conflict Transformation

John Paul Lederach is a sociologist by training and it may be considered unusual to cite his work in the development of a practical theology of reconciliation. He currently is Professor of International Peacebuilding at the University of Notre Dame and has engaged in the practice of peacemaking for several decades. While his academic preparation was in sociology, his motivation for the work springs out of his Mennonite background and the biblical vocation of peacemaking. Although he uses predominantly sociological language, he reflects on his experience from the tradition of his Christian denomination and the Scriptures and allows that reflection to inform his praxis. As such, he uses what I consider to be a practical theology methodology.

The work of John Paul Lederach has been as peacemaker and educator. He has extensive experience in working for peace in situations of war and large-scale societal conflict. He has drawn on his sociological training to develop an integrated framework to guide that work.[26] Here it is not necessary to present that complete sociological framework, which informs his praxis of peacemaking in situations of large-scale social conflict. Within that conceptual framework, however, is an understanding of reconciliation that is relevant. I will begin this section by outlining Lederach's concept of reconciliation; second, I will describe a related, yet distinct, framework of conflict transformation; and finally, I will present Lederach's concept of the moral imagination as an important capacity in the praxis of reconciliation.[27]

1) *Reconciliation*

The foundational activity of reconciliation is the building of relationships.[28] Two relevant assumptions are contained in such an understanding. The first is: "that *relationship* is the basis of both the conflict and its long-term solution. . . . This approach, though simple in its orientation, has wide-ranging ramifications: Reconciliation is not pursued by seeking innovative ways to disengage or minimize the conflicting groups' affiliations, but instead is built on mechanisms that engage the sides of a conflict with each other as humans-in-relationship."[29]

An important part of this understanding is that social systems must be looked at as a whole and the various parts are understood in terms of their relationships within that whole system. Lederach uses the image of a spiderweb to illustrate this interconnectedness.[30]

Second, reconciliation requires that the mutual exclusion of the "other" which is a result of conflict, must be broken down so as to create an encounter between the parties in conflict. "People need opportunity and space to express to and with another the trauma of loss and their grief at the time of the loss, and the anger that accompanies the pain and the memory of the injustice experienced."[31] For Lederach, the acknowledging that comes from having their story heard validates the experience and the feelings that accompany the experience and is a first step toward the restoration of the person and the relationship. At the same time, he writes that the encounter cannot be just about the memory of the past events, but must also include a way of envisioning a shared future.[32]

In regard to this encounter, Lederach creates an interesting image by describing reconciliation as being a place, specifically, the place of encounter where the past can meet the future. "Reconciliation is a locus, a place where people and things come together."[33] In a like manner, he identified the locus of reconciliation as a place where justice, truth, peace, and mercy come together. Lederach identifies this image as arising out of the use of Psalm 85 in a peace process in Nicaragua, the English translation of Spanish text used (verse 85:10) being: "Truth and mercy have met together; peace and justice have kissed."[34] In a later work, this image was developed into a narrative, called "The Meeting," that I have found useful in my ministry of reconciliation.[35]

Lederach summarizes his understanding of reconciliation in this way:

> Reconciliation . . . is focused on building relationship between antagonists. The relational dimension involves the emotional and psychological aspects of the conflict and the need to recognize past grievances and explore future interdependence. Reconciliation as a locus creates a space for the encounter by the parties, a place where the diverse but connected energies and concerns driving the conflict can meet, including the paradoxes of truth, mercy, justice and peace.
>
> Reconciliation as a concept and praxis endeavors to reframe the conflict so that the parties are no longer preoccupied with

focusing on the issues in a direct, cognitive manner. Its primary goal and key contribution is to seek innovative ways to create time and a place, within the various levels of affected population, to address, integrate and embrace the painful past and the necessary shared future as a means of dealing with the present.[36]

2) *Conflict Transformation*

Lederach makes another contribution to the foundational theory underlying the praxis of reconciliation through a framework that he calls conflict *transformation*. This is in specific juxtaposition to the more commonly used phrases of conflict *management* or conflict *resolution*. The change in language represents a significant shift in the approach of responding to conflict. It is a move away from an approach that seeks "merely" to resolve a particular issue. Rather, it is an engagement in constructive change efforts that seek to build healthy relationships and communities.[37]

Lederach offers this definition: "Conflict transformation is to envision and respond to the ebb and flow of social conflict as life-giving opportunities for creating constructive change processes that reduce violence, increase justice, in direct interaction and social structures, and respond to real-life problems in human relationships."[38]

As such, conflict transformation is more than a set of techniques, it is a set of lenses for viewing conflict, while recognizing in conflict the opportunity to create a response that can construct a new and better personal and social situation.[39] Lederach identifies three such lenses. First is the need to see the immediate situation, and second is the need to see beyond the presenting problem to a deeper pattern of relationship. Lederach calls these two lenses the episode and the epicenter of the conflict. "An *episode* of conflict is the visible expression of conflict rising within the relationship or system, usually within a distinct time frame. It generates attention and energy around the particular set of issues that need response. The *epicenter* of conflict is the web of relational patterns, often providing a history of lived episodes, from which new episodes and issues emerge."[40]

The third lens that conflict transformation provides is a conceptual framework that helps to connect the episodes and epicenters of the conflict.[41] Lederach constructs this analytical framework through inquiry into the personal, relational, structural, and cultural dimensions of the conflict. "In the broadest terms, the transformation framework comprises three inquires: The presenting situation, the horizon of preferred future, and the development of change processes linking the two."[42]

In summary, several points present within Lederach's framework of conflict transformation are worth highlighting:

1. Conflict is viewed as an opportunity to bring about a transformation of a conflicted social situation, creating one that reflects a peace that is based on justice.

2. The focus of the inquiry and the intervention is on the human relationships and the web of relationships present within the social system in conflict.

3. The starting point of such an intervention and the design of constructive social change processes is an analysis of the personal, relational, structural, and cultural aspects of the conflict.

4. "Conflict transformation suggests that a fundamental way to promote constructive change on all these levels is dialogue."[43]

5. The change process must simultaneously respond to the episode and epicenter of the conflict.

3) *Moral Imagination*

One other point that is important in understanding Lederach's conceptual framework of reconciliation and that can serve to transition into the next section on praxis is his concept of the moral imagination.

In his recent work, there is a shift in Lederach's writing as he shares his inner musing and reflections on his years of experience in peace building. In some ways, he seems to be stepping out of the constraints of his sociological discipline to express a more personal, artistic, and theological perspective. In *The Moral Imagination: The Art and Soul of Building Peace*, Lederach reflects on the following question: "Is building peace an art or a skill?"[44] The answer that he develops through this text is that it must be both. This is in contrast to what he has seen (and helped create) in the developing profession of conflict resolution and peace building, which is oriented toward technique and the management of the process. Without wanting to negate the need for skill and technique, he writes, "We must envision our work as a creative act, more akin to the artistic endeavor than the technical process."[45] What is needed he calls our moral imagination, which is the "capacity to imagine something rooted in the challenges of the real world yet capable of giving birth to that which does not yet exist."[46]

Contribution to Praxis

In *The Journey Towards Reconciliation*, Lederach writes about the praxis of reconciliation as he reflects on his own ministry of reconciliation. Interestingly, one section of this work deals specifically with my own pastoral concern, the need for reconciliation within the church. In this he reveals an approach that is guided equally by sociological and theological perspectives.

The story Lederach tells is of working with a congregation from his own Anabaptist Mennonite denomination.[47] He observes somewhat wryly, that while the Anabaptists have long held a "peace" stance, their history is full of conflict. Unfortunately, this identifies a commonality in all Christian denominations. He begins by noting that within churches, conflict is often thought of as sin. The belief seems to be that "if everyone just did what they were supposed to do, we wouldn't have this problem." As a sociologist he notes that the culture of most churches is not conducive to conflict transformation. Instead, often the operant culture is to avoid speaking of conflict, be nice, avoid confrontation, etc. He then presents an analysis of the effects or changes that conflict can have on a church if it is not dealt with effectively.

The pattern that he sees when a church is not able to effectively deal with conflict is one of escalation.[48] First the conflict becomes personalized as we tend to identify the problem with the other individuals with whom we are in conflict. We might ask the other: "What is your problem?" They often respond to such perceived attacks by raising new issues that they can use to confront us. This moves into a blaming game where the conflict becomes more personalized as we get more explicit in the accusation of blame for the cause of the conflict. As the conflict escalates, the language often becomes more and more general as we lose sight of the original issue. Now the conflict has become polarized as a conflict between "us" and "them." We then talk less with the other group; instead we talk about them within our own group. We talk almost exclusively with the people who agree with us as the boundaries and differences between "us" and "them" gets solidified. The conflict can take on a negative spiraling effect as we react to the latest outrage committed by the other side and we move even further from the original presenting issue. In the worst-case scenario, we decide that we are too different from them to remain in the same church. While describing this pattern in one brief paragraph may seem a harsh caricature, my own observations would support the validity of this general pattern.

For a ministry of reconciliation that responds to conflict within the church, Lederach goes to Scripture. His use of Scripture, however, is not strictly exegetical, in the theological sense of the word. Rather it is more of a social analysis of the pattern of interaction that he observes in the passages. He develops a model of a ministry of reconciliation through his reading of Matthew 18.

Lederach writes that, "Matthew 18 is a chapter about conflicts."[49] He notes that it begins with the disciples squabbling about who is the greatest and ends with a parable about money and payment schedules. In the middle, we find the passage on "fraternal" correction (vv.15-20). Because of the context of this chapter, Lederach purports that this passage is primarily about working for reconciliation. "We are called to work for the restoration and healing of people and their relationships."[50] Lederach reads this passage as practical guidance for the work of reconciliation and he outlines a pattern of that ministry in four steps.[51]

Step 1: Go directly.[52] The first step may seem obvious, but it is to go directly to the one with whom I am in conflict and to speak directly with them about the disagreement. While obvious, it is often the step that many are unable to do. It requires that the person not only acquire good self-awareness through their self-reflection but also have the prayerful vulnerability that leads to a spiritual discernment that allows them to then turn toward the other and engage them in a nondefensive manner. This "vulnerable transparency"[53] requires a spiritual maturity.

Step 2: Taking one or two witnesses along. Contrary to the more typical reading of this passage, which would suggest that the witnesses are to offer collaborating testimony of the wrong that has been committed in the conflict or to arbitrate a settlement, Lederach reads this as a call to create a forum for the work of reconciliation. As indicated in step 1, the primary responsibility for reconciliation rests on those who are engaged in the conflict. Therefore, the witnesses are needed to create a body of people or forum, which I would call a community, to help "discern what is happening and what needs to be done."[54] They are witnesses, not to the situation of conflict, but to the possibility of reconciliation.

Where "two or three are gathered" (18:18-20) has both practical and spiritual aspects. "On the practical side, this step concerns the development of capacities and skills that help create the safe place for people to be transparent and interact with each other. The spiritual dimension means that this kind of space is holy ground. It represents the place where we encounter God and each other."[55]

Step 3: Telling it to the church. Like step 2, this activity is to shift the forum and to bring the conflict to the even broader forum of the church. Again, the responsibility for the conflict rests on those directly engaged in the conflict while the church is to provide the assistance needed for that conflict to be addressed. For Lederach this step affirms that working on conflict is a spiritual activity and reconciliation is the mission of the church. He summarizes the spiritual dimension of "telling it to the church" as: "The people who make up the church and its very structure are living testimonies of working out the mission of reconciliation (2 Cor. 5:18-19). The church is a place of encounter. It is a place of Truth-discerning and Truth-telling. It is a place for vulnerable transparency. It is a place for interactive engagement. It is a place for accountability. It is, after all, a place where we journey towards each other and towards God."[56]

Step 4: Relating as with a Gentile and tax collector. Lederach observes that the usual interpretation of this instruction in Matthew is to read it as a mandate to avoid the sinner. Lederach relies on a simple theological principle of discipleship, however, which is to follow in the footsteps of Jesus by doing what he did; thus he asks, "How did Jesus relate to Gentiles and Tax Collectors?" The answer is that he ate with them, with all the implications of observing table fellowship in that culture. To eat with another was to establish or maintain a relationship. So, even if all else fails and the one in need of fraternal correction rejects the call to conversion and the discipline of the church, Jesus says to remain in relationship. Lederach continues by observing that in these relationships we follow the example of Jesus if we are able to:

- define ourselves without projection or retreat; accepting vulnerable transparency and encouraging it in others

- foster a nonanxious presence that is able to accept that others will define themselves differently and that we are able to engage those differences

- maintain the relationship and remain emotionally connected. Stay at table together.[57]

A Synthesis

In my ministry of reconciliation, I have long used a synthesis of the works of Robert Schreiter and John Paul Lederach. I have discovered that they have much in common and that their differences are more a result of the emphasis demanded by their academic disciplines than a divergence of thought. In this conclusion I list some essential commonalities that I find in their understanding of reconciliation and also highlight some differences, while claiming elements that I think are essential to a practical theology of reconciliation. In this I will integrate both theory and considerations of praxis.

In general, as a theologian Schreiter provides a clearer and more complete articulation of a theological understanding of reconciliation. Lederach is more the practitioner, and he arrives at what could be considered a similar theological position but does so through his reflection on his peacemaking experience. For Lederach, there has been a development of thought in his work, from a more strictly sociological perspective and praxis toward one that is more explicitly grounded in his faith life and theological beliefs.

For both authors, their understanding of reconciliation flows from a Christological perspective that equates the life and mission of Jesus with the mission of reconciliation. Schreiter provides the better articulation of this concept as foundational for his development of a Christian spirituality of reconciliation. While only elements of that framework are echoed in the work of Lederach, I find nothing in his work to think that he would not accept the five distinctive characteristics of a Christian spirituality of reconciliation.

Building on this Christological foundation, Schreiter makes an important assertion about the "vertical" and "horizontal" dimensions of reconciliation. Lederach is less explicit in making that linkage, but in his writing on the vocation of peacemaking he is clearly of like mind.[58] Here their difference may be one of emphasis. Schreiter frames reconciliation within the broader narrative of the paschal mystery while Lederach approaches it more practically within the methodologies of praxis that he offers. In this, Schreiter is asserting the place of God as the primary agent of reconciliation, hence the importance he places on the vertical axis and the need for a spirituality to guide the actions of ministers of reconciliation. Lederach is guided by a social construction orientation and leans toward an emphasis along the horizontal axis and the construction of the "new creation." While different, these two positions are more complementary than contrary and are certainly not mutually exclusive.

Both see conflict as an opportunity to encounter God and to create a more just situation. As a sociologist, Lederach places a high value on the need to analyze the conflict within the social system and to identify causes as a starting point in praxis. Especially in his earlier work,[59] he develops a highly detailed process for analyzing conflict and pursuing a peacemaking goal. On a less technical level, his later work on conflict transformation, especially the need to recognize and distinguish between the episodes and epicenters of the conflict, I have found to be useful in my ministry.

Both Schreiter and Lederach present reconciliation as a process and a goal. The goal arises out of their acceptance of the preaching of Jesus and in their praxis to arrive at that goal, both outline methodologies that are processes. In this, both place the emphasis on the restoration of relationships.

In their commendations for praxis, neither Schreiter nor Lederach claims to be presenting a how-to manual. Schreiter offers a reflection on Jesus' ministry of reconciliation, developed from an exegesis of the postresurrection appearance narratives. This simple methodological framework emphasizes the need for the pastoral accompaniment of victims of injustice as a means of allowing them to come to a place where they can experience the healing power of God. The "how" of that healing is attributed to the grace of God and the specifics of that ministry of accompaniment are not highly developed. The importance of community in the work of reconciliation, however, is highlighted as providing the space of safety and hope where the victim is able to share the narratives and memories of the trauma that they have experienced. In the telling and retelling of the narrative, the victim comes to remember the trauma in a new way and can be brought to a new and restored identity by God.

Because of its focus on large-scale global conflict and a detailed sociological approach, I have found the praxis contained in Lederach's *Building Peace* to be unhelpful in addressing my pastoral concern. Simply, I find the framework is too complex to adapt in my ministerial setting. His more recent work, however, which addresses a more familiar context, has much to offer and in these recommendations for praxis he has much in common with Schreiter. He also offers an approach that places the work of reconciliation within the activity of a faith community. In a similar way, he recognizes the need for victims to give voice to the injustice that they have encountered, and the trauma or source of conflict is a primary focus for the work. They both articulate an approach that addresses the conflict directly through truth telling. As previously noted, he differs from Schreiter in recommending a more practical guide for responding to the conflict and for creating a more peaceful and just situation. While not a how-to manual, the model of ministry that he developed through his reflections on Matthew 18 offers some clear signposts for the journey to reconciliation.

In his most recent work, Lederach has distanced himself from the more technical aspects of his previous methodology and has explored the artistic aspects of the ministry. In some way, this brings him more in line with Schreiter's assertion that the work of reconciliation is more a spirituality than a strategy. With the concept of the moral imagination, Lederach has introduced what seems to be an important idea, however its practical implications for a praxis of reconciliation has yet to be articulated.

For a ministry of reconciliation within the church, it is essential to be rooted in a solid theological understanding, as articulated by Robert Schreiter. A reconciliation ministry is a lived expression of a Christian spirituality. This needs to be balanced and augmented, however, by practical methods that have their origins in the social sciences. The work of John Paul Lederach provides some guidance in this regard. But even more, in the organizational theory of Appreciative Inquiry, we find a theory and an organizational change process that is effective for bringing about reconciliation and healing in a fractured faith community. That theory and process is described in the next chapter.

CHAPTER THREE

Appreciative Inquiry: Theory and Process

Appreciative Inquiry is based on a reverence for life and is essentially biocentric in character. It is an inquiry process that tries to apprehend the factors that give life to a living system and seeks to articulate those possibilities that lead to a better future. More than a method or technique, the appreciative mode of inquiry is a means of living with, being with, and directly participating in the life of human systems in a way that compels one to inquire into the deeper life-generating essentials and potentials of organizational existence.[1]

David Cooperrider
Positive Image, Positive Action

Shifting Paradigm

Appreciative Inquiry (AI) is a new way of viewing the world of organizations and human systems. In particular, it is a new way of thinking about organizational change and development. As such, it is best understood in contrast to the current scientific paradigm.

The prevalent theory of organizations has its roots in classical Newtonian mechanics. Newton sought to explain how bodies move in the universe and his theory constructed a model based on the assumption that the universe is like a vast machine. The image used is of a clock with many interacting parts. Each part could be isolated and thought of in terms of its mass and the forces that act upon it and cause its movement.[2]

"Newton's work and that of his predecessors led to a scientific paradigm that has dominated our view of what is real for several centuries. Frederick Taylor's early theories of 'scientific management' came out of that paradigm, applying the image of machine to a human system."[3] Margaret Wheatley describes the result of that in her work *Leadership and the New Sciences: Learning about Organization from an Orderly Universe*. Because we all live and work in organizations that are designed from a Newtonian image of the universe, she writes, "We manage by separating things into parts; we believe that influence occurs as a direct result of force exerted from one person to another; we engage in complex planning for a world that we keep expecting to be predictable; and, we search continually for better methods of objectively perceiving the world."[4]

In recent times, Newtonian physics has come under challenge by new scientific theories. Quantum physics, chaos theory, self-organizing systems and complexity theory have raised questions about the reductionism and determinism that is a part of the Newtonian model. These new sciences have as a common denominator a search for a theory of wholeness.[5]

> These "new sciences" give us a radically different way of making sense of our world. The most exciting ramification for the field of organizational change/transformation is the realization that organizations as living systems do not have to look continually for which part is causing the problem or which project is not living up to some set of criteria. The "new" science embraces the magnificent complexity of our world while assuring us that built into the very fabric of the universe are processes and potentials enough to help us and all organizations move towards our highest and most desired visions.[6]

The theory and practice of AI has its conceptual roots in the new sciences. While in the old paradigm an organization (or world) was considered to be like a machine that could be dismantled, analyzed, and put back together in a better way, the new paradigm presents an organization that is a living system constructed by the language that we use to describe it and that we experience in line with the images we hold of it.[7] This has particular significance for how problems are approached. "Appreciative Inquiry would seem to suggest that by *focusing* on the deficit, we simply *create more* images of deficit and potentially overwhelm the system with images of what is 'wrong.'"[8] The alternative approach, when faced with an organization problem or concern, is to focus on the positive.

Arising out of this new paradigm, AI is more than a new organizational methodology; rather, it "becomes a *way of seeing and being* in the world. In other words, when using the AI frame, we do not see problems and solutions as separate, but rather as a coherent whole made up of our wishes for the future and our path towards that future."[9]

Appreciative Inquiry Defined

> Appreciative Inquiry is a collaborative and highly participative, system wide approach to seeking, identifying, and enhancing the "life-giving forces" that are present when a system is performing optimally in human, economic, and organizational terms. It is a journey during which profound knowledge of a human system at its moment of wonder is uncovered and used to co-construct the best and highest future of the system.[10]

I wish to highlight certain aspects of AI that are revealed within this definition. The first is that AI must be understood as a process. As such, the definition of AI reinforces the idea that AI is a mindset or a frame of reference for looking at organizations. Methodologies and models of the AI process have been developed—an example of this will be detailed later—but the key point is that AI is a dynamic, not static, approach and that the breadth of the AI frame of reference allows for, even requires, great creativity in its application.

Second, it is "collaborative and highly participative." The bias present within the approach is to engage the whole of the organization. The broader the participation, the better the process. Again, this may be best understood in contrast to the approach that is more commonly employed. In the old paradigm, activities like planning and organizational development were viewed as the responsibility of those at the top of the hierarchical structure. Typically, senior or executive management of an organization, or the pastor of a church, would dissect the organization and redesign structures and operations to achieve the desired change. They would then advocate for their design and defend their plan as it met with resistance from the rank-and-file members of the organization. In contrast, the AI approach would call for the broadest possible participation of the stakeholders (both internal and external) of the organization to be involved in the "co-constructing" of the future.[11]

The DNA of Appreciative Inquiry

The essential components of the AI approach to organizational change are identified as five key principles and five generic processes. Jane Magruder Watkins and Bernard J. Mohr call this the DNA of Appreciative Inquiry[12] (appendix A).

1) *The Constructionist Principle*

The idea that a social system creates or determines its own reality is known as social constructionism. AI takes this theoretical framework and simply places it in a positive context. The positive spin on social constructionism is central to AI. Many of its principles flow from the idea that people control

> their destiny by envisioning what they want and developing
> actions to move towards it.[13]

This is an important theoretical soil for the development of AI theory and practice. A social system or organization is not fixed by nature, but is the product of a shared knowing and communication. "Knowledge about an organization and the destiny of the organization are interwoven."[14] In particular, the "reality" of an organization is determined by those who participate in the shared life, which gets expressed in the stories that they tell of the history and current life of the organization. Appreciative Inquiry is rooted in this principle in that it purports that by changing the shared narratives of the organization, the reality of the organization shifts.[15]

The role of narratives is very important in the AI process. Appreciative Inquiry theory holds that by changing the narrative it is possible to co-construct a desired future. "The most important resource for generating constructive organizational change is cooperation between the imagination and the reasoning function of the mind (the capacity to unleash the imagination and the mind of the groups). AI is a way to reclaim the imaginative competence."[16]

2) *The Principle of Simultaneity*

> Here it is recognized that inquiry and change are not separate,
> but are simultaneous. Inquiry is intervention. The seeds of
> change—that is, the things people think and talk about, the
> things that people discover and learn, the things that inform
> dialogue and inspire images of the future—are implicit in the
> very first question we ask. The questions that we ask set the
> stage for what we "find," and what we "discover" (the data)
> becomes the linguistic material, the stories, out of which the
> future is conceived, conversed about, and constructed.[17]

Often people find it hard to lay aside the myth of the old paradigm which says that organizational change begins with analysis and is followed by implementing a decision about how to effect change. Instead, the theory put forth by AI states that all inquiry into a social system is fateful; that is, the inquiry itself has an effect on the organization.

This principle has two significant influences on AI theory and practice. The first is that, although AI processes get described in a sequential order, the steps in the process must be understood as overlapping and individual actions can simultaneously be understood as an expression of multiple steps. Second, if our questions are themselves fateful, then our questions take on added importance. In the old paradigm, questions are used to gather information that is then used to design the intervention. But if we recognize that the questions themselves are interventions, then the crafting of the questions to be asked takes on significant importance. Cooperrider and Whitney write: "If we accept the proposition that patterns of social-organizational action are not fixed by nature in any direct biological or physical way, that human systems are made and imagined in relational settings by human beings (socially constructed), then the attention turns to the source of our ideas, our discourses, our research —that is, our questions. Alterations in linguistic practices— including the linguistic practice of crafting questions—hold profound implications for changes in social practice."[18]

The importance of the questions asked will be seen in two distinct yet related ways. The first is in solicitation of memory. The AI process is rooted in the collected memories of the organization. As will be described below, a first step in the process is to discover or remember the best of the past. It is through the questions that are asked that the memories are solicited and the participants are directed to identify the "best" of the past. The careful crafting of these questions is a key process success indicator because the memories that are solicited are the foundation for all the work to follow. Second, questions are important because they are used to stimulate the imagination. Imagination is needed and used to create a shared dream for the future. It is the stimulation of the imagination that energizes the participants and fuels the positive transformation of the organization. The organization is empowered and enlivened by the very process of asking carefully crafted and properly focused questions. With good questions, transformation is simultaneous with the asking of the question.

3) *The Poetic Principle*

> A useful metaphor in understanding this principle is that human organizations are an open book. An organization's story is constantly being co-authored. Moreover, pasts, presents, and futures are endless sources of learning, inspiration, or interpretation (as in the endless interpretive possibilities in a good work of poetry or a biblical text).[19]

An important implication of this principle is that because organizations are open books, we have complete flexibility in our choice of how and what we are going to study. We can study problems or we can study success stories. We can focus our inquiry on our disappointments or on our hopes and dreams. How that freedom is used is key to the AI theory and practice.

The "co-authoring of the organization's story" is another way of stating the social construction principle. The shift in language from "constructing" to "authoring," however, reflects the fluidity that will be seen in the process described below. "Constructing" would seem to indicate that there is a blueprint or engineering plan that needs to be followed in a structured way while "authoring" reflects the necessary creativity or continual improvisation that is necessary in the use of an AI process as it is tailored to the particular context in which it is being employed.

4) *The Anticipatory Principle*

The most important resource that an organization has for the coauthoring of its future is its collective imagination, which is given expression in the conversations and discussions about the future that occur within the organization. In this way, it is said that "the basic theorems of the anticipatory view of organizational life is that it is the image of the future, which in fact guides what might be called the current behavior of any organism or organization."[20]

Like a movie projected onto a screen, a human system continually "projects ahead of themselves a horizon of expectation that brings the future powerfully into the present as a mobilizing agent. Organizations exist . . . because people who govern and maintain them share some sort of discourse or projections about what the organization is, how it will function, what it will achieve, and what it will likely become."[21]

It is important to understand that this principle is not suggesting a magical or mystical connection between what we believe and what will occur in the future. Rather, it purports that the narratives that are told about the imagined future of the organization help to define and determine the identity (and future) of the organization because the stories that are told influence the interactions of the participants today. It is the actions of today that create the future reality. An example that illustrates this can be found in the religious congregation that tells and retells the narrative of their declining membership and their congregational dying, who then live that narrative into reality as they cease to invite new members or create new opportunities for mission.

5) *The Positive Principle*

Two experienced AI practitioners write: "Building and sustaining momentum for change requires large amounts of positive affect and social bonding—things like hope, excitement, inspiration, caring, camaraderie, sense of urgent purpose, and the sheer joy of creating something meaningful together. What we have found is that the more positive the questions that we ask in our work the more long lasting and successful the change effort."[22]

At the core of the AI theory and approach is that a positive future is constructed on the positive core that is present today within the organization. For this reason, those elements, characteristics, or events that are most positive about the organization become the sole focus of the process. This is a radical departure from the more common organizational dynamic approach of inquiring into the problem and designing a solution.

Cooperrider and Whitley write that the most important thing that their experience has taught them is that "human systems grow in the direction of what they persistently ask questions about and this propensity is strongest and most sustainable when the means and ends of the inquiry are positively corre- lated. The single most prolific thing a group can do if its aim is to liberate the human spirit and consciously construct a better future is to make the positive change core the common and ex- plicit property of all."[23]

The unwavering focus on the positive is essential in the AI process. The rationale for that is presented in the next section and will be revisited in the description of the AI process, which follows.

The Importance of Appreciation

When you bring together the anticipatory principle and the positive principle, you have the foundational theorem of AI; that is, positive images lead to positive action. There is solid research to support this theorem as the basis of an organizational change strategy. In his classic article, "Positive Image, Positive Action: The Affirmative Basis of Organizing,"[24] Cooperrider gives a more complete summary and cites that research, which I only briefly touch on here.

Medical research has shown that positive images, projected as a positive belief, have real healing power. Known as the placebo effect, "between one-third and two-thirds of all patients show marked physiological and emotional improvement in symptoms simply by believing in the effectiveness of the treat- ment, even when the treatment is just a sugar pill or some other inert substance."[25] Research continues on the mind-body path- way, but what can be demonstrated is that anticipatory images lead to real results or effects. Appreciative Inquiry incorporates the placebo effect into its theory by concluding that, like for an individual human, what a human system or organization anticipates and believes about its future, will have a concrete effect on the future that will be created.

Research into educational methodology has demonstrated the Pygmalion effect. Simply, teachers were told that a selected group of students had exceptional ability. In fact, the selected students were randomly chosen and had no greater ability than the rest of the class. In time, however, the selected students did begin to outperform the rest of the class, not because of any innate superior intelligence or ability, but solely because of the expectation that had been created in the teacher. "The key lesson is that cognitive capacities are cued and shaped by the images projected through another's expectations."[26] Because the teachers expected the selected students to perform better, they projected that expectation and the students responded to the positive image that the teacher had of them. This reveals a relational element in the positive image–positive action pathway and it has important implications for organizational leadership and for interventions that are motivated by a desire to transform a human system.

While not yet conclusive, some recent research has pointed to the link between the positive emotions that accompany positive images as a causal factor in the choice that a person makes to perform a positive action. "Somehow, positive emotions draw people out of themselves, pull us away from self-oriented preoccupations, enlarge the focus of the potential good of the world, increase feelings of solidarity with others, and propel them to act in more altruistic and positive ways."[27]

All human systems (and individuals) have a continual inner dialogue. Like an inner newsreel, the system is continually recounting the memories of the past and bringing various accounts of current and future scenarios into a dialogue that seeks to interpret and bring meaning to those events. That inner dialogue is influenced and expressed in the narratives (the outer dialogue) of the organization, but it is primarily an inner expression of the shared beliefs about the organization that are held by the participants and influences the unconscious choices of the participants. In that dialogue the human system brings into a dialectic both positive and negative statements and the outcome of that dialectic becomes the guiding image of the organization. Studies show that in healthy and effectively functioning organizations, there is a 2:1 ratio of positive to negative images. A mildly dysfunctional group might have an inner dialogue where the ratio of positive to negative is equal.

The AI process seeks to introduce positive images into the organization's inner dialogue. "The AI dialogue creates guiding images of the future from the collective whole of the group. It exists in a very observable, energizing and tangible way in the living dialogue that flows through every living system, expressing itself anew at every moment."[28] The use of questions within the process of AI is to influence the organization by guiding the dialogue of the organization toward positive images. Simply stated, if one is able to change the dialogue, one is able to transform the organization.

Sociological research also affirms that a positive image of the future has a dynamic influence on the organization. The Dutch sociologist Fred Polak held that the single most important indicator of the health of a social system and the most important variable in understanding cultural evolution, is found by observing if the system holds a positive image of the future. Simply, "when there is a vision or a bright image of the future, the people flourish."[29]

Based on a wide spectrum of research, AI has emerged to challenge a long-held paradigm of organizational theory. Appreciative Inquiry needs to be understood as a new frame of reference that requires a new model for working with organizations and for designing and implementing strategies to assist an organization to achieve a desired transformation. I turn to that model now.

The Appreciative Inquiry Process

Watkins and Mohr write that within the practice of AI, there are five generic processes for applying the underlying theory to a framework for organizational change. They are:

1. Choose the positive as the focus of inquiry;

2. Inquire into stories of life-giving forces;

3. Locate themes that appear in the stories and select topics for further inquiry;

4. Create shared images for a preferred future; and

5. Find innovative ways to create that future.[30]

These processes are called generic as a way of emphasizing their flexibility and the need to adapt them to specific situations or contexts. Part of the attractiveness of AI theory is that it supports and recognizes the uniqueness of each context and organization and practitioners are encouraged in facilitating change within an organization by adapting the practices used elsewhere. As opposed to *one* defined AI model, through the application of the principles and generic process in concrete situations, AI practitioners have developed several models that bring the generic processes to life. Through the collaboration of AI practitioners and a sharing of their work results, there has been and continues to be a progressive development in the practice of AI.

The original process model was developed in 1987 by the originators of AI theory, David Cooperrider (then a doctoral student) and Suresh Srivastva (his academic advisor). While their theoretical work began with a concern for how to approach the building of generative theory, it moved quickly into a process for intervening with groups. That original model was later adapted to create what has become the widely used model of AI practice, the 4-D Cycle (appendix B). While it is widely used, Cooperrider is clear that AI is more than the 4-D Cycle. "The cycle is simply a tool that allows the practitioner to access and mobilize the positive core. The positive core lies at the heart of the AI process. In this respect, the positive core is the beginning and the end of the inquiry."[31] A description of steps in the 4-D model will follow, but first we look to the important task of defining the topic of the inquiry process.

Choose the Positive as the Focus of the Inquiry

"To understand AI at a fundamental level, one needs to understand these two points. First, organizations move in the direction of what they study. Secondly, AI makes a conscious choice to study the best of the organization, it's positive core."[32]

Because an organization will move toward that which it studies, the choice of the topic is a critical first step. Watkins and Mohr writes that the AI process begins when the organization consciously chooses to focus on the positive. Because an organization is likely to act out of the old paradigm and to unconsciously choose to focus on the negative issue or problems that they are facing, it is the work of the AI practitioner to help the organization to identify a positive focus and to make that topic choice.[33]

"Selecting the affirmative topic choice begins with the constructive discovery and narration of the organizations 'life-giving' story."[34] While there is great room for variability, a typical AI process would be limited to three to five topic choices. Although those topics can be preselected by the practitioner in cooperation with the leaders of the organization, there is a strong bias that the topics be "homegrown" through a mini-AI process with a representative subgroup (topic selection team) of the organization. That process would be to *discover* what factors had given life to the organization when it was functioning at its best in the past and to begin to *dream* and *design* a vision for the future. That process with the topic selection team would be built around the following foundational AI questions:

- Describe a high-point experience in your organization, a time when you were most alive and engaged.

- Without being modest, what is it that you value most about yourself, your work, and your organization?

- What are the core factors that give life to your organization, without which the organization would cease to exist?

- What three wishes do you have now to enhance the health and vitality of your organization?[35]

Ideally the topic selection process would be a one- to two-day process. The goal is to work with the topic selection team, which can later become the steering team for the overall AI process, to foster dialogue and mutual deliberation. Using a mutual interview process that utilizes the questions listed above, data is collected and then in small groups the team works to identify common themes and formulate the positive topics for the AI process. While topics can be anything related to the goals and aspirations of the organization, they must meet the following criteria:

- Topics are affirmative and stated in the positive.

- Topics are desirable. They identify the objectives people want.

- The group is genuinely curious about them and wants to learn more.

- The topics move in the direction the group wants to go.[36]

4-D Cycle[37]

The Discovery Phase

"The primary task in the Discovery phase is to identify and appreciate the best of 'what is.' This task is accomplished by focusing on peak times of organizational excellence."[38] Using carefully crafted questions and interview guides, the participants enter into a process of mutual interviews in which stories of organizational accomplishment are solicited and recorded. Participants need to "let go" of analysis of deficits and systematically seek to glean from these stories of past accomplishment the core life-giving factors (leadership, relationships, structures, values, core processes, etc.) that contributed to those successes.

In this phase the power of storytelling gets unleashed as participants come to know their organization's history as the foundation for positive possibilities for the future. Through positive dialogue and the celebration of past success, hope and organizational capacity for effectiveness is heightened. Participants connect to one another through a dialogue of discovery and often the seeds for a positive future begin to emerge.[39]

The Discovery phase is for data collection and narrative exploration. "An important goal is to stimulate participants' excitement and delight as they share their values, experience, and history with the organization and their wishes for the future."[40]

The process itself has several key steps. It is necessary to identify the process participants, with a bias toward very broad participation. As previously noted, the questions to be used in the interviews need to be crafted to solicit the positive life-giving core. A guide is often needed to assist the participants in the interviewing activity. The method for doing the interview is determined by the situation. Often this is a mutual process, done one-on-one in pairs of participants at a process gathering.[41] A plan also needs to be in place to collect and organize the data from those interviews. Working with the data from the interviews is part of the work of the core team and is used to continue the definition and management of the AI process.[42]

The Dream Phase

"The *Dream* [phase] amplifies the positive core and challenges the status quo by envisioning more valued and vital futures. . . . The Dream phase is practical, in that it is grounded in the organization's history. It is also generative, in that it seeks to expand the organization's potential."[43]

The Dream phase takes the data, the narratives that were told in the Discovery phase, and "mines" them to imagine the possibilities that they contain for the future. Here the participants dialogue about the potential of the organization to achieve greatness in the future by building on its rich history. Ordinarily, this dreaming generates its own energy and enthusiasm in the participants and the sharing of dreams and generation of excitement is the first goal of the Dream phase. The second goal is to begin to identify the common themes that are present within the dreams. The necessary stance for the process remains appreciation, not analysis and judgment. The dialogue is not to identify the ideal dream for the future, but to continue the process of mutual discovery of the life-giving forces that contribute to the organization's success.

While the context and number of participants are determining factors, most of the work in this phase is done in small (<12) groups. Keeping together the two-person teams used in the mutual interviews of the Discovery phase, they are grouped with others to form "Dream teams." It is here that the "dream dialogue" occurs and common themes are identified. They create a shared picture or dream of the future, which they creatively (skit, story, picture, mock newspaper report, mock panel presentation, etc.) present to the whole group of participants.[44]

The Design Phase

While the Dream phase was involved with creating a macro-vision of the organization, in the Design phase the move is toward a more micro level of imaginative possibility. "The Design phase involves the creation of the organization's social architecture. This new social architecture is embedded in the organization by generating *provocative propositions* that embody the organizational dreams in the ongoing activity."[45]

An underlying step in the Design phase is to determine the elements that are going to be present in the social architecture of the organization. Examples of these elements are: leadership or management style, roles and relationships, organizational values, vision and purpose, operating processes, etc. The simple question that guides this phase is: What has to be in place for the organization to realize its dream?

"The Design phase defines the basic structures that will allow the dream (or vision) to become a reality. Like the other phases, the Design phase requires widespread dialogue about the nature of the structures and process. This is what is meant by co-constructing the organization's future."[46] For this phase of the AI process, participants are invited to work in self-selecting groups. Work group or Design teams are formed around the dreams that have been articulated, which in turn reflect the topics of the AI process. The freedom given to the participants to choose their area of interest ensures that energy is maintained within the work groups and contributes to the transition to the next phase.

This phase is "driven" by the writing of provocative propositions or possibility statements. The Design teams may begin with participants writing individual statements, but the goal is to arrive at shared statements. Always articulated in the present tense, these statements present a vision for the future by painting a picture of what the organization looks like when its positive core is being expressed in all aspects of the organization.[47]

A good provocative proposition stretches and challenges the organization, yet remains in the realm of real possibility. It points the direction for the organization to move from the best of "what is" to the best of what "might be." They represented the desired future of the organization, which is stated in bold, affirmative terms.

The Destiny Phase

The Destiny phase (sometime called the *Doing It* phase) takes the dreams for the future, which have been expressed and designed through the provocative proposition, and makes them a reality as the participants are "invited to align his or her own interactions in co-creating the future."[48]

The Design and Destiny phases are significantly intertwined. In an open space planning and commitment session, the Design teams present their provocative statements or vision for the future and ask for the support of those gathered. Individuals and groups discuss what they can and will do to contribute to the realization of the organizational dreams, which are presented in those provocative propositions. This creates a relational web of commitments that is the basis for future action. These self-selecting groups then plan the next steps for creating the social architecture required to sustain the institutionalization of the desired design.[49]

> This [Destiny] phase is ongoing. In the best case, it is full of continuing dialogue; revisited and updated discussions and provocative propositions; additional interviewing sessions, especially with new members of the organization; and a high level of innovation and continued learning about what it means to create an organization that is socially constructed through the poetic processes in a positive frame that makes full use of people's anticipatory images.[50]

The successful AI process results in a transformed organization. It creates an organization that has developed the competencies to sustain appreciative organizing. They are continually appreciating the best of their actions. They are willing to be self-challenging to achieve even greater life-giving possibilities. They have developed the ability to dialogue and collaborate in a manner that allows them to continue to cocreate a desired future and to continually be the author of the book of their organization. In short, they have become appreciative learning cultures that function in the new paradigm in accord with AI principles and practices.[51]

Before I move on I want to add one final note on the AI process. The 4-D model has become one of the standard approaches for using the AI process. Watkins and Mohr have modified the approach, however, to include a preliminary or initial phase. They have created a 5-D model by including a Definition phase. It is during the Definition phase that "the goals of the process, including the framing of the questions and the inquiry protocol, the participation strategy and the project management structure are developed."[52] I think that it is a significant modification because it embodies two key AI concepts: All questions asked are fateful, in that they have an effect on the organization, and the intervention begins (simultaneity) with the first question asked. Because of this, I think that my project with St. Agatha, which I will describe in the following section, began with the first conversation I had with the pastor of the parish, and the narrative in the next section will reflect this 5-D model.

Appreciative Inquiry Summit

The principles of Appreciative Inquiry and the change processes that flow from it can be implemented in many ways.[53] There is no one "best" way. Rather, it is determined by the situation of the organization and the goals that are desired. Nevertheless, the methodology of choice that is emerging is the practice of the AI summit.

An Appreciative Inquiry summit brings together a broad range of participants for a single event or series of events to implement a 4-D process or other AI method. As an alternative to an approach that would work with individuals of subgroups of the organization, with a series of meetings over an extended period of time, the summit finds its value in bringing together and involving all the participants in the process. Requiring much preparation, a summit is ordinarily three or four full days of engagement in the process. While this requires a significant commitment of time and resources, the return on the investment is that it strengthens relationships within the organization and it can quickly produce remarkable results.

In the next section I tell the story of the Appreciative Inquiry process that I led at a parish. As I will describe, we chose to modify and utilize an AI summit approach. In that situation, because our goal was to restore a sense of communion, we decided that we needed to use a methodology that brought the whole parish together to engage in the process. In his book *Memories, Hopes, and Conversations: Appreciative Inquiry and Congregational Change*, Mark Lau Branson tells the story of how AI can be effective using a progressive AI meeting approach. Through a series of meetings utilizing AI, he helped a Presbyterian Church respond to their situation and plan their future.

Appreciative Inquiry and Responding to Perceived Negative Events

As people first learn about AI theory and practice, they often question if AI can adequately respond to problems or negative events. The concern is that by choosing to always focus on that which is positive or life-giving, problems will not be addressed because the AI process "sugarcoats reality" and fails to tell the truth of the adverse situation. This is especially a concern when there is perceived injustice within the human system or organization.

To such concerns, Watkins and Mohr respond: "AI can be used to solve problems; it just approaches problem solving with a different perspective. Traditional problem solving looks for what is wrong and 'fixes' it, thereby returning the situation to the status quo. Appreciative Inquiry solves problems by seeking what is going *right* and building on it, thereby going beyond the original 'normal' baseline."[54]

Problem-solving strategies arise out of the assumptions inherent within the paradigm that we use to understand organizations and human systems. In the old paradigm that views organizations as finite systems, problems "need to be tackled" and injustice has to be confronted with the truth of justice, usually through an accusation of wrongdoing. If we hold to the theory that organizations are socially constructed, then the problem-solving strategy changes as we recognize "that both problems and resolutions are social constructions, created by our dialogue and generalized into social norms and beliefs. In this situation (using AI), resolution is generalized throughout the system and builds in the potential to move continuously towards our highest image of ourselves and our systems."[55]

In their book, Watkins and Mohr provide a case study of the AI process that was led with Avon Mexico. Avon Mexico wanted to respond to accusations of gender discrimination and sexual harassment. Instead of using a problem-solving approach that might have confronted the injustice of sexism that was inherent in the system, they began an AI process with the positive focus of valuing gender diversity. The process used the 4-D model and it transformed the organization, making it not only more profitable but also a national award-winning organization for having policies and practices that benefit women in the corporation. By recognizing that in every human system there are positive aspects that can be discovered and that can become the foundation on which the dream of a more desired organization can be built, problems are addressed.[56]

I would compare the AI approach to problem solving to the use of a lever to lift an object. When faced with the problem of lifting a five-hundred-pound rock, I can try to get my arms around it and (unsuccessfully) try to raise it up; or I can place a fulcrum and use a lever and lift the rock by pushing down on the lever. Just as focusing our efforts on the lever will accomplish the desired effect on the rock, by focusing on the positive and the life-giving aspects that are present within the organization, AI addresses the negative situation or problem.

In summary, AI responds to problems by approaching the problem from the "side" of the solution; by transforming the organization into the organization that it dreams it can be (without the negative situation or problem). Even in the most egregious inequitable situations, the "solutions" are embedded within the organization and they can be discovered through an Appreciative Inquiry of the positive life-giving forces that are present.[57]

Within the AI framework, effective leaders must have the necessary appreciative competencies to assist the organization to be an appreciative learning organization. Appreciative Inquiry is not just a change management tool. It is a mindset, a way for people to understand their organization, which guides human interaction within human systems. A primary task of effective leadership is to assist the organization to function within that framework. This requires participative management and a spirit of collaboration where all in the organization can participate in the dialogue that constructs an effective organization.

In organizations that are experiencing a negative situation, effective leadership is critical. In negative situations, an important leadership task is to manage the dialogue within the organization. Inquiry into the negative aspects of an organization must be done in a way that solicits positive data, which can assist in the transformation of the organization. Again, the case study of Avon Mexico is illustrative. When faced with concerns about gender inequality, the initial task was to shift the focus to the positive or desired alternative—valuing gender diversity. Instead of leadership searching for examples of inequality and assigning blame and demanding accountability, the AI process began with the discovery of the opposite: tell a story of when you have seen women and men working together effectively here at Avon Mexico. Those positive images were the foundation of their successful transformation into an organization that valued gender diversity.

While the case of Avon Mexico is an AI intervention, it reflects the same AI pathway that effective AI leaders will use in responding to conflicts or negative situations within their organization. The task is not to deny or "whitewash" problems as they are identified. It is not a Pollyanna approach that censors truth telling. Rather, rooted in a conviction that positive actions only flow out of positive images, a leader responds to a negative situation by inquiring: Yes, that negative situation exists; so what is the positive alternative that we desire? An effective leader responds by saying: What is our dream of being a better organization and what can we discover in our history to build that dream on? How can we design and live that dream of an organization into reality? Effective leaders do not deny negative situations. Rather, with an AI orientation, leaders transform negatives into positives.

The fracturing of a faith community is an extremely negative event, in both emotional and spiritual terms. A return to the faithfulness of communion requires pastoral intervention. Most forms of intervention focus on the negative impact of the underlying conflict and events that precipitated the distress in the community. Those who have been involved in such efforts can all describe that these processes are not only difficult and uncomfortable but frequently unsuccessful in affecting the healing that is desired. Appreciative Inquiry offers an alternative approach that is positive and that can bring about the restoration of communion. To that, St. Agatha Church in Chicago can give witness.

SECTION TWO

CHAPTER FOUR

A Community's Journey of Reconciliation: Walking in Faith and Moving Forward with Christ

Like all stories of ministry, this one begins with the recognition of a pastoral need and a desire to respond. The story of the sexual abuse of children by the pastor at St. Agatha Catholic Church had been prominently reported. As a chapter in this larger issue within the Roman Catholic Church, this story had a particular poignancy because it was a story of recent abuse and the failure of the Charter for the Protection of Children and Young People to offer the protection that it promised.[1]

The *Chicago Tribune* has told the story through multiple articles since the initial report of allegations against Father Daniel McCormack (January 22, 2006). It was an article on the appointment of a new pastor, however, that prompted my involvement. Father Larry Dowling was appointed pastor in February 2007. He succeeded an interim pastor who had served the church following the removal of McCormack in January 2006. In that article, Dowling is quoted as saying:

> "Now what is the task here? It's to bring healing. It's to continue to build on the good things here because there is still a

> wonderful core group of people here who have really stuck it out and want to see things continue to happen and continue to grow here. So, I want to help make that happen."

> "Some people say, We're ready to move on," Dowling added. "I also think that some people are still struggling with the 'whys' and the 'hows' did this happen. And that I have to sort out with them."[2]

Sexual abuse by a pastor has tragic effects in the lives of the young victims. The betrayal of trust also victimizes the faith community. While I share with all Catholics a concern for the children and young people who are victimized, and recognize the critical need for their pastoral care and our responsibility as a church to provide that care, it is the effects of that betrayal on the faith community that has been a focus of my personal pastoral concern. In Dowling's words I heard a similar concern as he began as pastor of that wounded church. I also heard in him a desire to assist the church to move forward by building on the good things present in the church, a pastoral approach that was consistent with the change theory of Appreciative Inquiry (AI). The newspaper article identified for me a need for a ministry of reconciliation and the potential opportunity of testing the use of a process of Appreciative Inquiry as a pastoral approach to facilitate the healing of a fractured community.

Commitment from Leadership

Dowling was receptive to my call and request to meet with him. Our initial meeting lasted over an hour and served several purposes. First, it was an opportunity for me to present myself and to express my pastoral concern for reconciliation within faith communities. I was able to briefly describe AI theory and my desire to test its applicability for promoting reconciliation and healing in communities.

Second, it was an opportunity to hear from him firsthand about his experience of coming to St. Agatha and his observa-

tions and hopes for the parish. He spoke fondly of the parishioners and with admiration for the depth of faith that he was
witnessing in the community. He also spoke of the effect of the
abuse allegations and the difficulty that followed in the parish.
He said that many parishioners had left the church and that the
2006 "October count"[3] was down about 45 percent from 2005.
Some parishioners felt that they were living under a stigma, with
neighbors asking them why they were going to "that church."
While many parishioners were angry with McCormack and the
Archdiocese of Chicago, others still believed that McCormack
was innocent. Dowling reported that while there were pockets
of continuing discussion of the case, attempts to discuss the
incident in the parish council were met with reluctance and with
their expression of a desire to move forward.

Third, in this initial meeting I also spoke of the elements of a
generic AI process. That led to a general discussion of what an
AI-inspired process at St. Agatha might look like. To that end,
I shared the 4-D model of an AI process (appendix A) and we
discussed how that might be utilized in the parish. That discussion led to an important decision: we would try to use an
AI summit methodology. Because Dowling had an underlying
desire to strengthen the sense of community in the parish, we
saw the value in gathering the whole parish together in one room
for the process. We wanted all to participate and have access to
the information that the process would generate and we wanted
all to be party to the decisions that would be made through the
process. Consistent with the principle of simultaneity, we wanted
to create a process in which the community would be relating
with one another in the desired unified way. While we recognized the difficulty that we would encounter as we tried to
gather the whole parish together for multiple sessions, we
thought that to use the summit methodology was a better choice
than an AI process that worked through multiple meetings with
individuals or subgroups of the parish.

An underlying concern that I had about the use of AI in a faith
community setting was the amount of time required for an

effective process. While there are ample examples in the literature about using AI with businesses, including nonprofit businesses, there are fewer examples of the theory being applied in settings like a church, in which all participation by the members is voluntary. A very important factor in determining the suitability of using an AI approach with a faith community must be the determination of the level of commitment to invest the necessary time. From the first conversation with Dowling, I wanted to be clear that this was not a one-shot, quick-fix approach and that a decision to move forward was to make a significant time commitment. I stressed the importance of trying to create the broadest possible participation and the important role of a core team to define and lead the process. My role was to be one of consultation and facilitation; I was not there to "fix" the situation.

Dowling was enthusiastic in his responses throughout this initial meeting and was supportive of going forward with the project. With the wisdom of an experienced pastor, however, he deferred a decision on this to the parish council.

While it was very important for the parish council to make the commitment to the process, it was not an easy decision to reach. Several weeks after my initial meeting with Dowling, I met with the council; however, that meeting was disappointing because only about half the council membership was present. It was never clear to me why the attendance was poor for that meeting. Nevertheless, I presented myself and my hope for being a part of an AI process at St. Agatha, covering much of the same ground as in the initial meeting with Dowling. I briefly explained AI theory and the generic AI process.

Appreciative Discernment

Like the initial meeting with Dowling, there was an element to this meeting of "selling" the idea of the parish using an AI process. To that end, I began to translate the ideas and concepts of AI theory into the language of the church. I baptized AI theory and christened it "Appreciative Discernment." While the origination and development of Appreciative Inquiry is found in the secular social science of organizational dynamics, it has been successfully utilized in many different types of organizations, including ecclesial organizations. My experience, however, has been that the language of Appreciative Inquiry is not comfortable to those in church settings. We have our own vocabulary. For that reason I decided that translating the theory into the language of the church would make the theory more accessible to church people. To that end, I began to speak about the process as Appreciative Discernment. I think that most members of a faith community have at least a basic familiarity with the term "discernment" and would see it as a spiritual activity; as a way of prayerfully making decisions about matters of faith.

The main point of translation of AI theory into church language is found in the questions used to explain the 4-D process (appendix C). For example, some guiding questions for the Discovery phase are: What gives life to the organization? What is the best of what is? Within a church framework of Appreciative Discernment, the guiding questions might be expressed as: How has God blessed us and been faithful to us? Where do we experience the grace and blessing of God? I believe that this sort of translation was beneficial in explaining the process and demonstrating its appropriateness for use with faith communities.

In my meetings with the leadership of St. Agatha, this was part of a successful effort to make the theory accessible to them by speaking of the theory in language familiar to them. It was a way of representing the AI process as a spiritual activity, a way for a church to be faithful.

Along with spiritual terminology, it was very important in the process at St. Agatha that we incorporate other essential elements of their religious identity. We used texts from the Scriptures and religious rituals throughout the process. (This will be described in later chapters.) AI theory has a foundational assumption that the members of an organization can create the organization that they envision according to *their* desires and values. For the community of faith at St. Agatha, this would mean creating a community that embodied faithfulness.

While the use of spiritual language helped the church leader-ship see the potential benefit of going forward with the process, after these initial discussions, I essentially abandoned the use of the phrase "Appreciative Discernment" in favor of speaking of the process in secular language. This project was my first experience of facilitating a full-blown Appreciative Inquiry process. In large part, my decision to employ secular language was motivated by my desire to be faithful to the principles of Appreciative Inquiry. Also, as an academic project, I wanted to be diligent in the citing of sources that are from the secular dis-cipline. While the decision to employ the secular language may have been appropriate for this project, in subsequent projects I have used the language of Appreciative Discernment as a way of emphasizing the process as a spiritual activity. When working with faith communities, I think that speaking of Appreciative Discernment helps to connect the process to the faith traditions of the community and makes it easier for the community and community leadership to embrace the process.

In my initial meeting with those members of the parish council present, they were supportive of the possibility of my accompa-nying the parish through this process, but they delayed a deci-sion because they wanted broader participation in that decision. It was decided that I would meet with a group of parish leaders to make my proposal. A meeting was scheduled for the next month, but was subsequently postponed.

A number of factors contributed to that delay. Most promi-nently was that on the day I was scheduled to meet with the leadership group, St. Agatha was again receiving media atten-tion. In a *Chicago Tribune* article that day it was announced that the contract of the school principal was not being renewed. She had been the principal at the time the abuse occurred. In the article, the principal linked the decision to terminate her employ-ment to her being critical of the archdiocese's handling of the abuse allegations. The archdiocese spokesperson denied the connection and said that the decision was based on the "current pastor's evaluation of her performance" and not related to past events.[4] Exacerbating the situation was that the decision was also featured prominently on local news telecasts. Regardless of the reason for the decision, it was another disturbance in the life of the parish, and I did not think that it was reasonable to expect the leadership team to focus on my proposal as this new event was unfolding. In fact, the parish leaders did meet that evening to discuss their current situation.

The issue of the principal's termination illustrates an important fact concerning the context of this project. The events that disrupted the harmony of the parish were continuing; it was not a *past* event. Further disruption occurred when McCormack entered a guilty plea and was sentenced to prison. Again this brought embarrassing attention to the parish and was a cause of distress. In the *Tribune* story of the plea agreement, Dowling noted that the plea agreement "helps the parish move towards closure. But that it also reopens old wounds."[5]

One result of the media coverage was that it continued to "label" St. Agatha as a place where children were abused and it presented an identity for the parish that belies their faithfulness. The publicity was a source of embarrassment for many parishioners who chafed at seeing their church characterized in this way. This was particularly true because of the involvement of a victim advocacy group that effectively brought media attention to the events of McCormack's offense and the manner in which they perceived the archdiocese failed in their response to the allegations. The victim advocacy group also demonstrated outside the parish when Cardinal George was present for the installation of Dowling as pastor. While I believe that all in St. Agatha Church seek to support those abused by their former pastor, many express a resentment of the advocacy group and think that they hindered the healing needed in the parish.

Definition Phase

While the meeting with the group of parish leaders was to present the proposal of St. Agatha using an Appreciative Inquiry process and to get their decision about the advisability of going forward, I treated the session as the beginning of the Definition phase of the 5-D process outlined by Watkins and Mohr. In part, this reflects my confidence that a positive decision would be made about going forward and that the group I was meeting with would become the core team for the process to follow. In fact, the pastor did subsequently appoint the participants of this meeting as the core team. It also reflects my concern about the amount of time that a good AI process requires and it was still unclear how much time the parish would be willing to commit to this process. So, while this meeting was to introduce parish leadership to the AI and to make the proposal, in some ways, I treated this session as the first step in working with the core team.

The group was invited together by the pastor and it included parish council members, representatives from the finance committee and other parish groups, and some staff. There were sixteen representatives present and we met for two hours. The starting point for the design of the session was the suggested agenda for an executive overview to AI found in the *Appreciative Inquiry Handbook*.[6] That outline suggests a way of helping an organization's leadership to become familiar with AI and to make the decision about pursuing an AI process. I modified the plan significantly, however, emphasizing the mutual interview exercise so that we would collect data that would be used to define the process.[7]

My desire going into the meeting was twofold: (1) arrive at a positive decision to go forward with the process and (2) gather information that would help the core team to define the process, specifically to help clarify the process purpose and the topics. Both desired outcomes were achieved.

Overall the meeting was enjoyable. It was apparent that the participants had warm relationships and cared about each other. They seemed open and forthright in their interactions and responses to questions. I was introduced by the pastor and he recalled how I had expressed an interest and had come to be there meeting with them. I began by giving a brief description of AI theory. There was some visible glazing over as I began with the theory and principles and I quickly moved to introduce the mutual interview process. Here and in subsequent processes that I have led, it has been clear that some experience of AI is essential to help people understand the value of the process.

For the interviews I simply had them find a partner and conduct the interview, using the interview guide that I had developed using the AI foundational questions (appendix E). The topic that I chose for the mutual interviews was the following: We're faithful, prayerful, and serving an awesome God. This was a quote from Deacon Greg Shumpert in the *Tribune* article on Dowling's appointment.[8] The interviews did generate information that we would use later to define the process. While there was skepticism as I introduced the mutual interview process, the interviews got them engaged and they were unanimous in recognizing the energy that was created. As we debriefed the interview experience, participants spoke favorably about the experience of hearing each other's stories.

I followed up the interview process with a description of the 4-D cycle of the AI process. Here again, I decided to speak about Appreciative Discernment as a way of highlighting that I was offering to accompany them through a spiritual process—this was not a strategic planning process but a discernment of faithfulness for the parish. As we discussed possibilities of how the process might unfold at St. Agatha, there was growing appreciation for the possibilities that the process offered.

I ended this session by articulating what I believed to be the key success factors for the process. In some ways this was a kind of pep talk. In my role as facilitator I always tried to model the positive attitude and behavior that is a foundational principle of the theory. I spoke of the necessity of our believing that God is ever faithful and that St. Agatha has been powerfully blessed and has the promise of a faithful future. As parish leaders, I asked for their commitment to positive participation and to being vocal advocates for the process. I outlined the responsibility and the work that the process would require of them, but promised that the investment of their time would result in the transformation of their parish. They "got it" and made the commitment to go forward.

Working with the Core Team

The Definition phase of an Appreciative Inquiry process is critical to its future outcome. Most essentially, because the desire is to bring about sustainable change within an organization that self-manages and is not consultant dependent, working with the core team that is composed of organizational leaders is a time of teaching and reinforcing the principles and practices of AI so that it can be the continuing operant approach in the organization. I was very conscious of this in my work with the core leadership team of St. Agatha and I facilitated their work in a manner consistent with AI theory and practice. This also highlights the importance of the work of the core team and my relationship to that team.

It was important that the pastor and the core team accept responsibility for the AI process. My desired role was to serve them as consultant to facilitate process design and the process itself. Time constraints had an important influence on my role, however. A recurring element of my work was to monitor the time demands on the core team and the parish. In this, there was a constant tension between what was ideally desired (as articulated in the literature and illustrated through the case studies presented) and what was practical in the context of a parish in which all participation is voluntary. The result was that I needed to assume responsibility for some process definition elements that might have ideally been more the work of the core team while also assuring their ownership of each step in the process. This is illustrated in the first definition task, the definition of purpose and identification of topics.

Defining the Purpose and Topic Selection

Defining the process purpose and topic are critical. August 7 was the first meeting of the newly constituted core team. Before, they had gathered as parish leaders to make a decision about going forward with the process; now they had accepted responsibility to be the core team. I began this session by reviewing and articulating the process in spiritual terms, as an Appreciative Discernment process, and I described the important role that they would play in the definition and leadership of the process. I described the effective working of the core team as being the key success factor for the process. We then set out to define the purpose of the process. I explained that we wanted to be able to define the purpose in a six- to eight-word phrase that would effectively name the process and assist us in communicating with the whole parish. Agreement on the purpose is also foundational to the working of the core team, as further development of the process would be determined by the purpose.

To do so, I asked the questions: What is your hope about this process? What benefit do you hope will come out of it for the parish? I then asked them to discuss these questions in groups of three persons. After a few minutes, each triad reported and I listed phrases and themes that were present in those reports. A sample of ideas that emerged are:

- strengthen the faith of the community

- plan for evangelization

- establish a clear mission

- draw on the gifts of the whole parish and build on those strengths

When we began to draw on the list of themes to write a purpose statement, however, we encountered our first difficulty. While there was a great deal of general agreement on our purpose and the desired outcome, we had difficulty in agreeing on an actual phrase to articulate that purpose and to name the process. After more than an hour of discussion, with some frustration evident, someone suggested that we table this issue until the next meeting as a way of giving people time to think and pray about it. So we decided to discontinue the wordsmithing activity and move to topic selection.

To begin this activity I explained how topic choice is a fateful act because the topic would be the focus of our inquiry and dialogue; as such, the parish would move in the direction of the topics we selected. Using the work of David L. Cooperrider, Diana Whitney, and Jacqueline M. Stavros as a reference, I described that a good topic would be an affirmation of the church's strength and potential. I asked the question: What are the important areas of the life of the parish that we want to dialogue about as a parish? Because of practical considerations, I said that we would need to limit this process to three to five topics and that those topics must meet this criteria:

- Topics are affirmative and stated in the positive. [To state the topic in the positive means to state the topic as if it were already the reality.]

- Topics are desirable. They identify the objectives that they want for the parish.

- Topics need to be something about which they genuinely want to learn more.

- Topics need to express the direction that they hoped the parish would move.[9]

For this activity, we utilized the information gathered in the mutual interview process of the previous meeting. While it would have been desirable for the core team to review completely the data from the mutual interviews and to identify themes, instead, because of the time constraints, I merely read the list of "essential elements" they had identified from their mutual interviews and asked them to identify themes from that listing.[10]

The interviews had generated an impressive list of attributes that inspired their pride. They had spoken of the warm hospitality and welcoming nature of the parish. They were proud of their African American heritage and the openness to people of other cultures. They recognized their deep faith and valued their spirited worship. Many spoke of the connectedness they felt with others in the parish and the support they offered each other.

Reviewing these attributes prompted a fruitful discussion, during which we brainstormed possible topics and captured those ideas on newsprint. Toward the end of the discussion, one participant tried to summarize the discussion by suggesting these three themes:

- Faith-filled and Spirit-driven

- Nurturing and supportive relationships

- Building community (This idea was about growing the parish through invitation and outreach into the neighborhood.)

While the discussion was fruitful, the meeting ended without a purpose statement or topic selection.

Two weeks later the core team reconvened to continue these two tasks and to begin our discussion of the process activity. I had done much preparatory work with the hope of arriving at a decision on purpose and topics. I began by outlining the tasks for the evening and saying that we needed to continue the important task of defining our process purpose and selecting topics. I said that we wanted to come to a consensus but that we define consensus as arriving at a decision that everyone is "OK with and can actively support." This definition seemed to help the group in the work that followed.

I began by saying that the purpose statement needs to answer the question of a parishioner: Why are we doing this? We wanted a statement that would be positive and inspire others to want to be a part of the process. Next, I explained that I had used my notes from our previous discussion and had drafted ten possible purpose statements, which I then read to them. Possible purpose statements:

- A faithful church/people moving forward together with Christ

- Celebrating what is and claiming what can be through Christ

- Charting a course into the future for a loving and vibrant church

- A faithful church claiming a vibrant future

- A vibrant and faithful church moves into the future

- Blessed, faithful, and moving forward (with Christ?)

- Drawing on (Claiming?) our blessings and discerning a faithful future

- Vibrant and Spirit-filled (or faithful?)—today and tomorrow

- This far by faith and going forth

- Being church—now and always

With that list in mind, we began to "mix and match" phrases and elements of the different statements and drafted a half dozen other possibilities. New ideas emerged, among them:

- Grounded by faith; growing together in Christ

- Anchored by faith and moving forward with Christ

- Founded in Christ and moving forward in faith

- Walking with Christ and winning by faith

After much discussion, we arrived at consensus on this purpose statement: *Walking by faith and moving forward with Christ.*

In the end, it was the journey motif that seemed to capture the imagination of the participants and expressed the desire of the participants that the parish could move beyond the effects of the betrayal that they had suffered at the hand of McCormack. Also, it was very important to them that the process be clearly identified as a faith activity; what we were going to be doing was the work of committed disciples discerning their path of faithfulness. In the weeks ahead this purpose statement served the process well in that it became a constant reminder of the reason for the work, and it was frequently incorporated into the inner dialogue of the parish through the conversations of parishioners and the worship of the parish.

We then reengaged the discussion of topic selections and the need to focus our inquiry. Again, I hoped to facilitate arriving at a consensus by drafting some suggested topics, from a synthesis of our previous work. After reviewing the characteristics of good topics, the topics I suggested were:

1. A vibrant and Spirit-filled church.

2. We are one: united and strengthened in Christ.

3. Being church after church.

By way of explanation, I connected them to the three topics suggested in our last meeting. The first topic would be to inquire about the worship and faith life of the church. The second would be a more inward focus and would solicit stories about the relationships that parishioners had with each other as a faith community. This topic would include the idea of being welcoming and hospitable, two attributes that they had "discovered" in the interviews process and believed to be essential to their identity. And finally, the third topic would bring to the process an outward or mission focus and would be an inquiry into the place of St. Agatha in the neighborhood and the ministry of the parish beyond worship. This would also be a way to explore the work of evangelization.

Initially, there was little reaction to my suggestion, positive or negative. The discussion seemed to lack energy. My concern was that I was exerting too much influence and that I was determining the topics for the process at the expense of allowing the team to truly control the direction of the inquiry. I expressed my concern about this and a team member responded by saying that to her the topics seemed obvious and that there was no need to comment. Others quickly agreed and all expressed that these were topics they would like to see be the focus of the process. While I continue to wonder about the way we arrived at the topics, I think these three topics—worship, community, mission—can be a useful guide for other parishes or faith communities if they are planning a similar AI process.

While they are expressed in ways unique to St. Agatha, they did reflect three basic or typical elements in the life of any parish. These three elements are, in fact, relationships. The first topic reflects the vertical relationship between God and God's people. The second topic is focused on the horizontal relationship that the members of the community have with each other. The third topic is about the relationship the faith community has to the world in which it is situated. In all the faith communities I have worked with since St. Agatha, these three relationships have been expressed in some way in the topics that we have used.

The phrase used to express the mission topic, "Being church after church," has the additional value in that it is a long-standing slogan used in the parish and has been incorporated into their worship dismissal rite. In the Roman Rite the customary dismissal rite has the celebrant or deacon proclaiming: "The Mass is ended, go in peace." And the congregation replies: "Thanks be to God." At St. Agatha the proclamation is left open-ended: "The Mass is ended let us go and . . ." And the congregation responds: "Be church after church. Thanks be to God."

With the purpose defined and topics selected, the last task of the evening was given over to my outlining the overall process. I spoke of my concern about the time commitment that would be needed but said that I thought we needed to commit minimally to three afternoon sessions. In general terms, I defined the purpose of each of those sessions, referring to the 4-D process that would serve as a framework for process definition. Stating the importance of "whole system" involvement, I asked them if they thought we could get a broad cross section of the parish to make such a time commitment to the process. They were thoughtful and serious as they considered and discussed the question, and they decided that a three-session process would be possible. We established a schedule for the process and, at my suggestion, split the core team into two groups: one would be responsible for the practical details of the process and the other would work with me further in process definition and session leadership. The team members chose their area of work and we set dates for future meetings.

Core Team Work Continues

A subsequent meeting with the part of the core team dedicated to the practical concerns was fairly short and to the point. The main focus of the meeting was to look at ways to facilitate whole system involvement. All agreed that broad and active participation would be best achieved through direct, personal invitation. Who to invite became a topic of discussion. I asked them to identify the "stakeholders" of St. Agatha, which was a term that required explanation. I suggested that we consider inviting anyone that we thought had an interest in the welfare of the parish. Of course, that would be active parishioners, but I also inquired about inviting inactive and former members, non-parishioners who receive service from the parish ministries, neighborhood representatives, archdiocesan representatives, etc.

While the pastor was enthused about the possibility of an expanded invitation list, in the end, the task of inviting the active parishioners seemed to be the focus of the effort.[11] They thought that through telephone invitations it would be possible to get 100 to 150 people to participate. I thought that this number was optimistic because that would equal the number of worshipers present on the two times I had attended the ten thirty Sunday liturgy.

This team also decided that youth, age fourteen and older, would be invited to participate fully, babysitting would be provided for those younger, lunch would be catered, name tags would be used, and a variety of other practical and important details.

Developing the Interview Guide

The subsequent meeting with the part of the core team focused on the process was equally effective. The purpose of this meeting was to define the first session and the materials that would be needed. The majority of the time was spent going through the interview guide to be used (appendix F).

Using a good interview guide is essential to a successful process. According to Watkins and Mohr: "What we ask determines what we find. What we find determines what we talk. What we talk determines what we imagine together. What we imagine together determines what we achieve."[12]

An interview guide needs to have a preamble that sets the tone for the interview and needs to summarize the project as a whole. In the guide we developed for St. Agatha, this was an opportunity to emphasize the spiritual motivations for the project. Often an interview guide is structured around three sections. The first is to set the context for the inquiry and begins to set the stage for the sharing of stories that discover the positive that is present within the organization. In this section there need to be questions that solicit stories of best experiences and the inherent values present in the organization and its people. The second section brings the interview to focus on the specific topics that were chosen. In some ways these questions are the heart of the interview because they gather the information that will be used to move the organization forward in a specific direction. And the third section draws the participants' attention to that future. Here it is particularly important that the questions be open-ended to allow the participants to engage their imagination and to identify the preferred future.[13]

Some version of the foundational questions are used in the interview, but the guide must be customized with carefully crafted questions. The crafting of questions is an important task and is guided by the positive principle that is foundational to AI theory. Questions need to be stated in the affirmative and invite the telling of stories. Questions are not to solicit facts or opinions. Rather, they are used to draw out of the person the values that are important to the person and the aspirations that the person has for the organization. The questions are to help the person identify and appreciate the positive aspects of the organization and imagine how those positive traits can be the foundation of a desired future.

In the project at St. Agatha, I drafted and proposed an interview guide for our use. While we discussed questions individually and they were modified during this meeting, the final draft was basically what I had presented. In that, we diverged from a more recommended process development theory, which suggests that this activity is preferably part of the core team's responsibility. Perhaps a better interview guide would have been developed through the collaborative writing by the core team, but the time needed for that would have been extensive.

While the core team never balked at any request that I made on their time, attendance by individual core team members fluctuated. In this situation, that is to be expected. The practice of Appreciative Inquiry, as described in the literature, is labor intensive. In this project I needed to make decisions regularly as to how to minimize the time demand without minimizing the effectiveness of the process. Often the decision that I made was to accept more responsibility for the process definition tasks, with the hope that it did not undermine the needed commitment and investment of the core team in the process.

Another meeting of the full core team was held the week prior to the first session. This meeting was to review again the plan for the session and to continue to animate the team members to make the calls and to build interest in the session through their invitation of the parishioners.

The Definition phase of the process was a very labor-intensive effort. The core team and I did a lot of work. Once a decision was made to go forward, we were able to focus and accomplish what we needed to do in about six weeks, meeting four times as a group. Outside of the meetings, much work needed to be done to invite the participants and to handle the practical details of the parish sessions.

CHAPTER FIVE

Discovery: How Has God Blessed St. Agatha Church?

Pre-session Preparation

The first session with the parish was on Sunday, September 16, 2007. It was a beautiful, sunny day and the presence of approximately ninety parishioners represented a significant level of participation. The participants were almost entirely from the roster of current active parishioners, and I think it demonstrates the effectiveness of the work of the core team to individually invite people to participate. Also important was the work of building anticipation for the process through church bulletin announcements and the pastor's speaking to the importance of the process on previous Sundays. The demographics (age, gender, etc.) of the participants appeared to reflect the parish: more women than men, but a significant number of men; more elderly than youth, but there was also participation of teens and young adults.

While the work of the session was from one o'clock to four o'clock, in effect the session began with the celebration of Eucharist at ten thirty. This is the "main" liturgy of the parish, with the largest number of congregants and is the most spirited worship service because of the participation of the gospel choir. Following the liturgy, a simple lunch was shared by those staying to participate in the work session. All the activities (Mass, lunch, and the work session) were held in the same space (parish hall). The parish does not have a church building or space that is dedicated solely for worship.

The framing of the work session in this way had two significant effects and it was a pattern that we followed in subsequent sessions. First, it clearly situated the process as a spiritual or faith activity; this was an activity of a church exploring their faithfulness. Second, the sharing of lunch provided positive affect, strengthened the sense of community, and affirmed the positive relationships within the church.

Each Sunday, the homily made specific reference to the process and encouraged the participation of the congregation. I believe that this served as a public endorsement of the process by the pastor and deacon and added to the legitimacy of the process in the minds of the parishioners. This eucharistic liturgy is always a spirited event, which is a source of pride to the parishioners; it built positive energy, which carried over into the rest of the session.

The sharing of the meal was also a boisterous and enjoyable time, much like a family reunion. The decision to have a meal together was guided by practical considerations. The pastor and core team had decided that the best time to gather a large group of the parishioners was on Sunday afternoon. But we knew that if people left after Mass to eat lunch, some would not return for the work session. The parish has a history of gathering for potlucks and barbeque picnics, but for this they decided to have a simple meal catered from a local supermarket. The effect of the Mass and meal was that we began the work sessions with a group that was already engaged with each other and with much enthusiasm for the work that we were going to do.

Creating an environment that generates the positive affect is a very important consideration in planning a process. An AI summit should be fun! This is not planning as usual. Fun activities are not just ice breakers but have an effect on the ability of people to engage their creativity and imagination. It allows the participants to engage in the process in a more holistic way, not just as rational beings, but as people who also have emotions and concerns that are important to them. The AI process provides a way for the members of an organization to bring their own "best selves" to the process of creating the best and most desired organization possible. For St. Agatha, having a meal together was a great way to begin the session. During the sessions, we also found creative ways to maintain that positive affect and to generate positive energy for the process. I will describe what we did as the story continues, but what we did at St. Agatha are just examples. As a core team defines the process that they will use, they need to engage their own imaginations and creativity in creating a fun and beneficial process for their organization.

The physical environment for the process is also important. The literature offers many examples of ways that attention to the environment can help set the stage for a successful process. Some of these descriptions can be a bit intimidating and well beyond the means of a typical church. In *The Appreciative Inquiry Summit: A Practitioner's Guide for Leading Large-Group Change*, a valuable resource on which I relied heavily, the authors describe an idealized setting for a process that includes the use of high-tech equipment and the use of materials and toys to help invite the creativity of the participants.[1] They describe a process with a corporation that was able to dedicate significant resources to their planning project. Most churches will probably lack these resources; they certainly were not available at St. Agatha. The lack of resources did not, however, prevent us from having a successful process. At St. Agatha we used what was available— the parish multipurpose room; chairs set up auditorium style and without tables so that we would have the flexibility to move around and to configure the participants into groups; stick-on name tags; we did not use PowerPoint presentations or any technology. It was fine. When I have led similar processes in other places, we did make use of technology and had more resources to utilize than at St. Agatha, but a lack of resources did not hinder the process at St. Agatha.

Integrating Prayer into the Process

It was a decision of the St. Agatha core team that the work sessions be designed to emphasize that this was not "just" a planning process but the church actively engaged in a spiritual process of discernment. To that end, each session followed a familiar prayer service format. We began with a liturgy of the word: call to prayer, opening prayer, reading of a Scripture passage, and reflection. The liturgy of the word was left open-ended so that it flowed into the work of the session. The effect was to invite the participants into the work as a continuation of the prayer. We supported this idea by incorporating prayer into the work session activities. We ended the work of the session by returning to the familiar format: Lord's Prayer, closing prayer, blessing, and dismissal.

Discovery Session

The first parish-wide session was focused on the discovery activity of the AI process. The presented goal for the session was: *How has God blessed us? Discovering what gives life to St. Agatha Catholic Church.*[2]

The pastor initiated the work session with some preliminary comments of welcome and a description of how and why the decision had been made to convene for this process. In those remarks he also introduced me and explained how I came to be involved, and that my involvement was part of my academic program and a pastoral concern that flowed out of my religious identity as a member of the Missionaries of the Precious Blood and our spirituality and charism of reconciliation.

These opening comments by the pastor were very important to the process. Called a "sponsor statement,"[3] it helps to focus the participants on the importance of the task at hand. It also serves as a personal invitation to the participants from the leader to be actively engaged in creating the future of the organization.

The session then began with a prayer service. Dowling planned the prayer service, but the choice of Scripture flowed out of the discussion of the core team in our preparation. For this session the Scripture passage used was the story of the disciples on the road to Emmaus (Luke 24:13-35). In his reflections on the Scripture passage he did an excellent job of connecting the journey motif expressed in the purpose statement: Walking in faith and moving forward with Christ. He also fulfilled my request that he share his personal hopes and dreams for the parish, which he believed would flow from the work they would do together. In summary, he acknowledged that the parish had been through a difficult time, but that the time had come for the parish to move forward. While the parish had been damaged by the betrayal of the previous pastor, God had not abandoned them. They may be confused by past events, like the disciples on the road to Emmaus, but they were a community of faith who together could discern the presence of God in their midst, and together they could respond in faith. It was a very hope-filled message in which Dowling provided leadership to his community in a straightforward manner. His leadership and clear ownership of the process was an important factor in the success of the session. The pastor was leading and the parishioners were ready to cooperate and participate fully in the process.

The Role of Facilitation

An important consideration throughout my working with St. Agatha was maintaining a role of facilitation that reinforced the autonomy of the parish and the important leadership roles of the pastor and others. I was not there as an expert to "fix" the parish. While my role was one of very active involvement and leadership of the process, I was not there to become the leader of the parish. Each of the three parish sessions was designed to recognize and support the pastor as the spiritual leader of the parish. The pastor and the core team were leading the parish in the spiritual activity of discernment; I was there to assist.

The need for an outside process facilitator remains an open question for me. Clearly, the one facilitating the process needs to be well-grounded in the theory of Appreciative Inquiry. Appreciative Inquiry is not a paint-by-numbers process. At St. Agatha, and the other faith communities that I have worked with, it has been necessary to be guided by the underlying theory as we found creative ways to progress through the 5-D cycle of the process. This is particularly true since most of the literature available on the practice of Appreciative Inquiry does not directly deal with the uniqueness of working with organizations like faith communities where there are time constraints because all participation is voluntary. That said, I think it could be possible for a well-prepared pastor to lead his church through this process.

As we had planned, in the prayer service Dowling left his reflection open-ended and allowed me to continue it. The purpose of my comments was to briefly introduce Appreciative Inquiry and to give an overview of the process we would be following. The goal was not so much that they acquire an understanding of AI as that they be reassured that the journey we were undertaking did have a road map and that what we were going to do this day fit into an overall plan. I used the Appreciative Discernment framework to describe the overall plan and I articulated the process purpose and the topics that we would explore.

In my description of Appreciative Inquiry I spoke for only fifteen minutes and I stressed only two points:

1. the social construction principle with its inherent promise that any future we can imagine, we can create

2. that an organization would move toward that which it most consistently talks about; so we were going to talk about the positives of St. Agatha, not the negatives

The social construction principle is very consistent with the Christian message of hope that all things are possible with the help of God. My talking of this was only a reinforcement of what the participants believed and a continuation of the message from their pastor. In my emphasis on the need to maintain a positive focus, I bluntly acknowledged the difficulty created by the wrongdoing of Daniel McCormack, but said that we were not there to talk about his action and its effect on the parish. Instead, in this process we were going to talk about the blessings that St. Agatha Church had received and their hopes and dreams for the future. The process was about moving forward in faith. As I made these comments, there was a visible sense of relief in the faces and posture of many of the participants.

Mutual Interviews

The heart of this session was a mutual interview process. The first step in this was to have the participants pair up. I did this in a simple way by asking all to stand and to find someone in the room that they did not know very well and who was different from themselves. When they found a partner I asked them to join hands and raise them so that I could know that all had a partner. This instruction was met with some looks that said, "What have I gotten myself into?" But the participants followed the instructions and the pairings were relatively diverse in age and gender.

I had the pairs of parishioners find seats together and we distributed the interview guides (appendix F) and the interview summary sheets (appendix G). I then gave some instructions for conducting the interviews. I began by reading the preface to the questions, with some comments to emphasize the importance of narratives as holders of truth and as containing the power to inspire. I told them that they would each have a turn as interviewer and interviewee. Then, specific to the activity, I invited them as interviewers to be curious, to use the interview guides and to make notes on it as they did the interview, but I emphasized that their task was to help their partner tell their stories. After conducting the interview, they were to use their notes and fill out the interview summary sheet. When they were being interviewed, I invited them to use this as an opportunity to give witness to the way God has blessed them and, especially with the dreaming questions, to free up their creativity. I asked them to give themselves permission to dream with audacious hope; to be like a little child who hasn't yet acquired that inner adult voice that says, "That will never happen." For the process I suggested they "be like a four-year-old who 'still' believes that anything is possible with God," an image that made many of them smile. Most of all, I invited them to have fun with the interview and not to get "hung up" on any particular question. At the very least, this was a chance to come to know a fellow parishioner better.

The interview guide that we used was carefully crafted as described in the previous chapter. Most questions included a brief "preface" that helped to explain and put the question into context. The guide began with some simple and safe questions to help establish a relationship between the interviewer and interviewee (here I am summarizing; see the interview guide in appendix F for the complete questions utilized):

- How did you come to join St. Agatha? What attracted you to the church?

- What are some of the activities that you are involved with today?

We continued with the foundational questions that had been customized for the process at St. Agatha:

- Tell me a highlight story of your involvement at St. Agatha.

- We know that we have received many blessings from God that make us who were are as a parish and we want to carry that positive core into the future. What qualities, traits, or characteristics do you see in the parish that we need to be sure to carry into the future?

- Can you share three gifts or blessings from God that you have received and that you bring to St. Agatha?

We included questions that addressed the specific topics we had determined would focus our inquiry:

- We are a vibrant and Spirit-filled church. Tell me a story when a worship service, a day of prayer, or a sermon really touched you.

- We are one: united and strengthened in Christ. When did being a parishioner here feel like "family" to you?

- We commit ourselves to *"Be church after church."* Please share a story where you have lived that commitment.

- How is St. Agatha, as a parish, *Being church after church* in our neighborhood?

And finally, the interview guide asked the parishioners about their dreams for the future of the parish. The interviewees were invited to imagine that they had been away from the parish but had returned to rejoin it in 2015, and they are amazed at the changes that they see in the parish. They were asked to describe what they see when they look at the new St. Agatha.

- What does our worship look and feel like?

- How are we relating to one another as a community?

- What impact is St. Agatha having on the neighborhood?

A final interview question asked the interviewee to share three prayers that they had for the parish. This is a variation on the foundation question that asks the person to make three wishes. This question reflects the adaption of the process to the religious process of Appreciative Discernment, but it serves the same purpose. Answers to this question reflect the areas of the parish that the interviewee considers most important. As such, they provide valuable information to be used in articulating a vision or dream for the future of St. Agatha.

Each interview was conducted in about forty-five minutes with a short break between the two interviews. During this time

I circulated among the participants answering questions and clarifying the activity where needed. The interaction that I witnessed was personal and focused. A later review of the interview guides affirmed that the questions were well constructed to elicit stories and most of the guides had notations from the interview. The summary sheets also were used effectively, although some were more detailed than others and a few were not used.

While the interview process was successful in discovering the blessings present within St. Agatha, some participants did find the process difficult. While few in number, these participants seemed to fall into two categories. The first group had literacy issues and were unable to use the form. In our planning, the core team recognized the potential difficulty of this, but we did not have a good way to respond. We did not want to single out people by asking them to identify themselves, so we decided we would treat the issue in a matter-of-fact way and in the instructions given I simply asked that the pairs of people assist each other. A second group included some people who had difficulty with the dream question (see appendix F, question 1 in section 3). Because this was only a few of the participants, I don't think the problem was with the question or the instructions; this is a foundational AI question that has been used effectively in some form in many, many situations. Rather, I think that some people had difficulty with imagining themselves in the future, seeing and describing what St. Agatha had become.

Bringing the Discovery Together

We ended the session with a small-group process that was designed to carry the group into the next session. As I circulated during the interviews, I gave each pair a number, which assigned them to a small group. The interview pairs had scattered about the large room. As I circulated and assigned them to a small group, I was usually able to assign the pair to a group that would be led by a core team member who was near them. This allowed me to point out the team leader to them, although most of the St. Agatha participants knew each other by name.

We formed nine groups of ten persons each. I had the participants gather in their assigned small groups and arrange their chairs into a circle. (This movement was facilitated by not having tables in the room, although I have also used the same gathering exercise in rooms with tables.) I then gave instructions for their group activity. My emphasis was placed on the fact that the groups we were forming were the small groups they would work with in the next session; in effect, they were being formed to become "Dream teams." Group leaders had been previously selected from the core team and they had been prepared to lead this activity.[4]

The group leaders introduced themselves and led the Prayer to Consecrate a Sacred Space (appendix J). Praying together and performing this simple ritual (people sign themselves on the forehead, lips, ears, and heart) was designed and included in this activity to emphasize the spiritual and communal nature of the process and to forge a connection among the small-group members. Group members were then asked to introduce their interview partner, using their notes from the interview guide. After all had been introduced, the group leader led them in a discussion to choose a name for their group. And as a last step, the group leader collected names and contact information for their group. They made two copies of the list; one that they kept so they could contact their team members before the next session and encourage them to be present at the second session and the other was collected by me to be a record of participation and to assist the parish in any follow-up activity that might be determined.

The names for the groups were mostly religious in nature. For example, the Miracle Workers and the Twelve Disciples were two of the names. The reason for the naming exercise was to strengthen the bond among the group with the belief that the stronger their sense of connection to the group and the work that the group would be doing, the more likely they would return for the second session. It seemed to have that effect with some friendly comments between the participants about who had chosen the best name. In a simple way, it was also an exercise of creativity, encouraging some imaginative dialogue among the group.

In general, the small groups were also animated and focused. The core team members who were leading the sessions had been well prepared and they all seemed to accept easily the role of leadership. They reported that the process of sharing the interviews was readily accepted by the participants and that group members were attentive to the stories that were shared.

I briefly wrapped up the session by summarizing what we had done and describing the Dream phase, which would be the focus of the process the following Sunday. The session was then concluded by Dowling with his thanks and with a very brief dismissal rite and blessing, similar to the conclusion of Mass.

Throughout the session, the engagement of the participants was evident. They maintained eye contact, looked interested, and readily followed the directions that were given. As the session ended I felt good about the start of the process and about the likelihood that the level of participation would continue in the work to come.

After the session, I met briefly with the small-group leaders to collect a copy of the participant lists and to remind them that we had a core team meeting on the following Tuesday to process the data and to prepare for the next week's session. To that end, I asked them to review the interview guides and summary sheets and to identify themes that were present. I also asked them to begin to imagine how the individual dreams of their team members might be woven into a collective team dream.

Core Team Follow-Up

The core team met on the Tuesday evening after each session for the purpose of appreciating the previous session and planning for the next. Watkins and Mohr refer to the appreciative approach of evaluation as "valuation."[5] In this biocentric or life-affirming approach, which is consistent with the underlying principles of AI, only the positive is given attention. In a traditional evaluation approach I might have asked: What did we do well and what could we have done better? With the core team, however, my questions were: What did we really do well? What do we want to be sure to do again next week? Was there a life-giving moment in the process for you? This valuation approach was new to the core team, but they did respond to my inquiries. While not quantifiable, it seemed to me that the team became more comfortable with this approach over the next two uses.

In response to the valuation questions they reported that they were pleased with the attendance and the depth of participation that they witnessed. They valued the way the process was facilitated and thought that aided the group to work effectively. They affirmed the decision to frame the process in spiritual terms, saying that the beginning prayer allowed them to enter the process through familiar territory. All thought there was great energy in the room and many were impressed by the way the parishioners embraced the process, particularly the instruction to pair up with someone unlike themselves; several people expressed surprise at some of the pairings they saw. Time seemed to go quickly and they appreciated how the interviews helped people to be open to each other. Several identified as life-giving moments the opportunity to hear the faith story of another, which inspired them and buoyed their spirit. The storytelling also energized people.

Overall, the pastor and the core team were happy with the start that the parish had made and were eager to engage in the preparation for the dream session the following Sunday.

CHAPTER SIX

Dream:
St. Agatha's Faithful Future

Pre-session Preparation

The core team met for two hours between the first and second sessions. Following the valuation process, we began to prepare for the next session by doing the human knot exercise. In the human knot exercise everyone stands together in a tight huddle and they are asked to raise their right hand and join right hands with someone else. Then they raise their left hand and join left hands with someone else, so they are holding hands with two other people. The result is a human knot. Then, without releasing each other's hands, they are instructed to untangle. It is a fun exercise and is usually full of laughter, but it does demonstrate a serious principle: with cooperation, perseverance, and a little humor, the knotty problems that make being together difficult can be untangled. An untangled human knot forms a circle.

The reason for doing the exercise that evening was to teach that principle, but more, it was to test the exercise as a way of beginning the Dream team exercise in the next session. The core team agreed that it would be fun to do and would likely have the same effect as it had with them, which was to invigorate them. The one caution was that some of the elderly participants or those with mobility issues might be enlisted as coaches for the exercise and not be included in the exercise directly.

Following that exercise I reviewed with the small-group leaders from the first session the themes and life-giving elements that had been identified in the interviews. Together, they generated a list of twenty (appendix K) that included traits such as:

- perseverance
- church is family
- care for our children
- openness to change
- seriousness about faith

I explained that these "gifts" would be posted around the hall to serve as visible stimulation for the dreaming activity of the next session. Together these themes pointed to St. Agatha's positive core and they represented the building blocks for the future that we would be dreaming of in the next parish session.

The rest of the meeting was dedicated to preparing for the parish session. I reviewed with them the outline for the session, with an emphasis on how they would be leading the small-group process. We went through the small-group leaders' guide in great detail (appendix L). The core team needed the opportunity to imagine what the session was going to look like and to raise their points of concern. Taking the necessary time for this preparation allowed the core team to be comfortable going into the second session and ready to exercise their leadership role.

While I met with the small-group leaders, Father Dowling met with other core team members to address practical issues for the session. The core team meeting ended with all feeling good about the first parish session and excited about what the following Sunday gathering would be for the parish.

Dream Session

The second session of the Appreciative Inquiry process at St. Agatha was on Sunday, September 24, 2007.[1] The guiding theme for the day was articulated as: *Dreaming: What awesome future is possible with the grace of God! Discerning the invitation and call of God.*

It was again a beautiful day, both sunny and warm. The celebration of the Eucharist was spirited and well attended. In his homily and in his other comments, Dowling referenced the afternoon session and encouraged participation. Following the lunch, about seventy-five persons stayed to participate. Of these, about six or eight had not been a part of the first session. Around the parish hall, which is also used for liturgy, the various "gifts" that had been identified by the core team in their review of the data from the first session had been printed on individual sheets of paper and posted.

The work session began with prayer (same pattern of prayer used in the first session) led by the pastor. The scriptural text chosen was, 1 Corinthians 12:4-11. In his reflection, Dowling made the connection of the Pauline text on the variety and unity of gifts with the listing of gifts that was up on the walls. He left his reflection open-ended for me to continue.

In my remarks, I recapped the previous session, noting that it had been an opportunity to hear the witness of another and to discover the ways in which God has been and continues to be present in the church. I also read off a sampling of the gifts that had been posted and referred to them as a rock or secure foundation on which to construct a church.

I then described our task for the afternoon. I briefly touched on themes that would support the work to be done. I spoke of the power of positive images to draw us into a positive future and that in talking about our dreams we were already beginning the journey to making them our reality. I reminded them that, as a church, our inner dialogue professes the belief that God keeps the promise made by Jesus that the Spirit will be with us always to guide us and that God has the power to change death to life. No death is final; no problem is beyond the healing of God. Finally, I encouraged them to free up their creativity and to dream big dreams. First, I recalled the quote from Daniel Burnham: "Make no little plans; they have no magic to stir men's [people's] blood."[2] Then I asked them: What is the dream that can stir our blood? What is a dream that we can give our lives to and is worthy of the gifts that God has given us? I explained that our work that afternoon was to allow the Spirit of God to give us a vision that would allow St. Agatha to thrive.

Finally, I invited them to allow their inner four-year-old to come out and play, and in groups of fifteen or twenty, we did the human knot exercise. It generated a lot of energy. Some people needed to overcome their reluctance to participate, but mostly people entered into the play. One group was unable to untangle and that too was positive, and there was lots of good-natured teasing. Generally, it seemed to have the desired effect of generating energy and opening people up to being creative. I mentioned that the purpose of the exercise was to help all to realize that at times our life together, like the work we were about to do, can be difficult and we can get all tangled up. At those times the temptation is to disengage from others and to give up. But that exercise demonstrated that by hanging on to each other and with a good measure of humor and perseverance in working together, it is possible to arrive at the circle of community that we desire.

Working in Small Dream Groups

We then reconvened into the nine small groups we had formed at the first session. These "Dream teams" formed small circles where their group name had been posted, along with extra news sheets. Participants who had not been present for the team formation exercise of the previous session were incorporated into the existing groups. This allowed the groups that were smaller because of the absence of members to be supplemented.

The task of this process was to explore the individual dreams of the participants and to develop a dream shared by the group.[3] To introduce the process, I began by giving some brief instruction on the criteria necessary for writing a good dream narrative.

A good dream narrative has to meet a specific set of criteria.[4] First of all, it is important that the dream be truly desired. This may seem obvious, but the danger here is that a church may select a dream they think they "should" adopt. Of course, as a church discerns its faithful future, it must remain mindful of the gospel message and the teachings of Jesus that have the weight of "commandments." A vision or dream statement cannot be a static interpretation of the Scriptures but must be reflective of a true desire (and commitment) to direct the future of that particular church in a way that reflects a discernment of the will of God in its particular circumstances. Unless the vision reflects the inner heart of the congregation, the congregation will not be committed to living that vision into reality.

Second, a dream or vision for the future needs to be bold and provocative. A vision has to reflect a reality that is not yet realized. It has to be more than an articulation of the status quo, even the status quo that reflects the best of who and what the church is today. A vision statement is that positive image that leads to positive action, that image of the future that can pull the organization or church into its desired future.

While it is necessary for the vision to be bold and provocative, a third criterion is that it must be grounded in reality. Within an Appreciative Inquiry process, dreaming is not fantasizing. The discernment of the vision for the future begins in the discovery of the ways that God has blessed us as a community. The vision is our answer to the question: If we use the gifts that we have received from God to the fullest, what would it look like? So, while a vision stretches the community beyond the present, we should be able to point to present evidence that the community has received from God the gifts needed to live that vision into reality.

And finally, a good dream narrative is unconditionally positive and stated in the affirmative. That means that the dream is written as if it is already a vision that has been realized. We place ourselves into the future and describe what we have become and what we are now doing. Practically, this means that it is written in the present tense, using active language. For example, a good vision statement would be: Through an effective evangelization program our community continues to grow by one hundred families a year. Contrast that statement with: We believe that we are called to evangelize so we are open to new members. Which statement has the power to inspire a congregation to action? I would hope that every church would say that they are open to new members, but a church that has a vision of growing by one hundred families each year has a positive image that can bring those new members to the church. It is a vision that brings the congregation to the task of developing and implementing an effective program of evangelization.

Following the brief instruction on what constitutes a good dream narrative, I gave some brief instruction for the process they would follow and the small-group leaders took over. The high energy from the human knot exercise carried into the group work. As I circulated among the groups I saw that the there was focused interaction. The process was led by the core team members using the small-group leaders' guide that had been developed. Going around the circle of group members, each of the individual dreams was recalled and developed. First, we asked the person to share the dream that they had been told by their interview partner the previous week. Then the team leader gave the person whose dream had been recalled a chance to add to their dream. The team leader asked questions to help the person develop their dream, questions like: What does our worship look like in your vision of 2015? In your vision of St. Agatha in 2015, do we have some new ministries that we don't have now? Once that individual's vision had been explored, the process continued with the next person, until all in the dream group had the opportunity to share their hope and vision for the future. Once all the dreams from the mutual interviews had been shared, those participants not present at the last session were given an opportunity to share their dreams. Those in the group who had not been present for the interview were asked by the team leader to share their vision, as well. The dreams of those not present, but who had shared a dream in the interviews of the previous session, were also read. While these could not be developed further, they were part of the overall picture being presented. Once all the dreams had been presented, the core team member leading the process facilitated a discussion in the group by asking two questions:

1. Of the dream stories we have heard, what most engages your imagination and gets you excited about the future?

2. Of the dreams we have heard, what are the key elements we want to be sure to include in our common dream?

The responses to the second question were recorded on newsprint to be used to write the group's dream narrative.

From Individual Dreams to a Group Dream

Following a break, the dream groups returned to the list of common elements and constructed a shared dream narrative. Here the goal was not necessarily to arrive at a consensus vision as much as to identify and include the dream ideas that generated energy and excitement within the group. The goal here was to write a narrative, not just list the elements. The reason for this is that narratives have the power to inspire and engage the imagination in ways that a listing of characteristics is unable to do.

At St. Agatha we had nine small dream groups and the experience in the groups ranged in effectiveness. Some groups were able to engage in dialogue, discussing the various key elements that had been identified and arriving at a statement, with relative ease. Other groups struggled to arrive at consensus. Some groups had more balanced participation than others. But in the end, all were able to write a vision statement.

The final small-group activity was to prepare to present their group dream to the full assembly of the participants. The dream groups were asked to present their dreams in a creative way, before reading the narrative. This use of presentations was a way of continuing the engagement of the imagination and fanning the flames of creativity. It helps the organization to see the vision of others, which facilitates the next step in the process of arriving at a common vision or dream for the parish. Probably as important as anything, the presentations prove to be a fun exercise with lots of laughter and spontaneous affirmation.

While it was not a difficulty at St. Agatha, with other groups I have encountered resistance to the idea of doing these presentations. To some groups the idea seemed "silly." Core team members have been afraid that the participants will not be willing to engage the process in this way. It can also be time consuming, depending on the number of groups that have been working. While these objections are sometimes raised in the planning, I can only affirm what is claimed in *The Appreciative Inquiry Summit: A Practitioner's Guide for Leading Large-Group Change*: "Finally, we have never yet had a group of people who, once into the flow of the summit, did not want to do the creative presentations. In fact, the preparation and delivery of the creative presentations invariably prove to be the highlight for people, both during and after the summit."[5]

At St. Agatha these presentations were very much a highlight of the process. Two examples will serve to illustrate this activity. One presentation was an enactment of a group of St. Agatha parishioners visiting a philanthropist to "make a pitch" for his financial support of the parish dream. It gave them an opportunity to speak to the various elements that were envisioned. A second example was a roving CNN reporter visiting and interviewing various parishioners of St. Agatha, asking them why the parish had been selected to receive a parish of the year award. This exercise allowed the participants to present their dream as they bragged about its fulfillment.

Following the presentations, I wrapped up the work of the session by noting the great amount of common elements that I had heard. Many of the participants nodded their agreement to this observation. While it was not possible in the afternoon session at St. Agatha, a recommended activity is to allow the participants to gather back in small groups to discuss the presentations and to "enrich the dreams."[6] The purpose of this activity is to solidify the dream and the commitment of participants to move forward by talking about the images that inspire them.

While the time constraint of the process at St. Agatha made that impossible, I shared my observations of the presentations and went on to list some elements that I had heard repeated. I noted features like:

- evangelization and the desire to grow the size of the church

- concern for the neighborhood and justice ministries

- Spirit-filled and vibrant worship with a choir that they were continuing to be proud of

- a welcoming and inviting spirit

I reminded them that we would meet again in two weeks and that while in this session we had gone from ninety individual dreams to nine group dreams, that before we met again the core team would repeat the process we had used and would take the nine dreams and construct *the* parish dream.

Coming to one common dream or vision is not always necessary. The important consideration in the Dream phase is to open up the organization to creative possibility and positive images that can draw the organization toward a positive future. The hope is to inspire people to create energy and new activity within the organization. The work of coming to consensus has the potential of bogging down the process, but at St. Agatha, where the goal was to effect reconciliation and restore communion, we decided that to arrive at a common vision was essential.

As the dream session ended, I let the parish know that the work of arriving at the common vision would be the responsibility of the core team. That would be presented to them at the next session as the vision for the parish's future. There it would be discussed, but most important, the next parish session would be a time where all would be given an opportunity to help to begin to realize that vision. I ended my comments by thanking the participants for their work and asking them to give themselves a hand and to express their appreciation for the core team as well. At that point, Dowling called the assembly to prayer and led the blessing and dismissal rite.

Core Team Follow-Up

The core team met again on the Tuesday evening after the session. We began by appreciating the session on Sunday and my asking, "What did we do well?" First of all, they valued the creative presentation of the group dreams, remarking that the groups enjoyed that activity. Just recalling the activity brought smiles to the faces of the core team members. All noted with some pride the good turnout and the investment of the participants. One person mentioned being asked by an enthusiastic parishioner, "When do we meet again?" Someone noted that the parish was blessed with many *committed* parishioners. I think that this observation, while not a new idea, reinforced the commitment of the core team members to the process we had undertaken. It was clear that all saw the value of the work the parish was doing and were anticipating the next steps. The human knot exercise was also viewed positively. It had been a humorous and fun activity that had generated a lot of positive energy that carried the group into the work of the session.

I asked, "What did you see that was really affirming of St. Agatha?" A core team member spoke of specific examples where they saw the youth being affirmed. Others remarked on how much the parish seems to have in common. Again the commitment of the parishioners to the parish was noted.

Finally, I asked if we had learned anything through the session that we would want to be sure to keep in mind going forward. To that there was wide agreement that we want to always give "voice" to the people. While this question and response was specific to the AI process that we were engaged in, the learning from the process had implications beyond the process. The positive approach of AI and its bias toward whole-system involvement was recognized as a preferred way of interacting as a parish going forward.

Arriving at a Shared Parish Dream

Following the valuation process we began by continuing the work of that session. Our task was to take the nine dream narratives from the parish session and create from them a common dream for the parish. I had posted on the wall the nine group dreams that had been recorded on newsprint at that Sunday's session. I then began to lead the process to arrive at a common vision by reminding them of the criteria for a good dream statement.

Once we reviewed the criteria, we read through the nine individual dreams that had been posted. The core team member who had led that group was given an opportunity to comment on the dream and the discussion in their group. As we read the nine group dreams, we listed important themes on newsprint, posted for all to see. When all the dreams had been heard, we looked to the list of important themes and began to prioritize and look for common elements. Working from that list, we then began to cowrite a dream that could serve as a vision for the future of St. Agatha.

It didn't work! As in a previous attempt to cowrite, while we seemed to have a high level of general agreement, we got bogged down in finding the language to express that commonality. There were over a dozen core team members present and all were invested in the process. That investment came with a strong desire to write the "perfect" narrative that would capture the dreams of all present and the groups they each represented. Drafting a narrative in a group that size is often difficult, and, in this situation, a different approach was needed. As we neared the agreed upon ending time for our meeting, we asked that a writing team of the pastor and two others work together to draft a dream statement that would capture our discussion. They agreed and it was decided that we would see if we could come to consensus via electronic communication prior to the next meeting.

The meeting the following week was more productive and it needed to be, as this was the last meeting to prepare for the third parish session. The writing team had done good work and had circulated a draft of a parish dream, soliciting comments. We began this meeting by reading and discussing their draft dream statement (appendix N). We made some minor modifications, but the work that the writing committee had done was recognized and appreciated. Returning to the definition of consensus that we had used before, to be okay with the decision and willing to actively support it, the core team affirmed it as a vision that met the requirements of a good dream statement. This was a dream that was desired, bold, and provocative enough to inspire the parish to move forward, while being achievable by building on the current giftedness present in the parish. With that important and unanimous affirmation, we moved into the details of the final session.

CHAPTER SEVEN

Design and Doing It: How Will St. Agatha Live the Dream into Reality?

Pre-session Preparation

With the agreement reached on a dream statement, the core team needed to prepare for the final session, a combination of the Design and Destiny/Doing It phases. A key activity in this is the writing of provocative propositions, which precedes and focuses the design activity. Ordinarily, as Appreciative Inquiry summits are described in the literature, these proposition statements would be a work product of the full group of participants, or minimally the work of the core team. If time permits the writing of provocative propositions in the work of the full group, that is certainly preferable. It will bring more creativity to the work. At St. Agatha, however, where we were conducting a summit in three afternoon sessions, we did not have that time available. I was faced with the need to compromise on process definition to arrive at a process that could be effectively implemented.

Working from the parish dream statement and drawing on the many discussions of the core team and the two parish sessions, I drafted a set of six possibility propositions.[1] Prior to the core team meeting I did ask the pastor to review the possibility propositions and he thought that they captured the essential elements of the dream and would appropriately focus the Design phase. I presented the propositions to the core team and they too approved them with only minor modifications.

The importance of the possibility propositions is found in that they are the specific focus of the Design phase. The six propositions which we adopted each expressed an essential element of the parish dream. Like a dream statement, they are rooted in the positive core that is already present within the community and they are expressed in a way that challenges the community by presenting a vision for the future that will stretch the parish beyond the current reality. By focusing the design efforts on these specific six elements of the dream, the design task is broken down and becomes more manageable. It also allows the participants to focus their own work in an area where they are interested and willing to invest their efforts.

Once the core team had arrived at a set of possibility propositions, we began to prepare them for their leadership role in the next session. There are different possible methods that can be used for the Design phase. Watkins and Mohr draw a distinction between approaches that involve whole system design and those that are based in individual action.[2] Their stated bias is for the whole system approach, which is more in keeping with the AI principle that seeks to encourage broad organizational participation. These approaches can also be rather complicated and be a process of organizational mapping of the key structures, activities, and relationships that comprise the social architecture of the organization. In the St. Agatha process, however, time constraints required that we adopt an individual action approach in which the participants are given an opportunity to make a personal commitment to act in some way that helps the parish to live their vision or dream into reality.

At St. Agatha I proposed that we use an individual action approach that made use of open space technology. Developed by Harrison Owen, open space technology is a method to facilitate individual participation in a group process.[3] In the process, people are invited to work in self-selecting groups and bring their personal contribution to the work of the group. While this method is used for many types of meetings and gatherings, it works particularly well in an Appreciative Inquiry process because it is philosophically congruent with the principles of AI.

With their approval of the possibility propositions, I asked the core team members to indicate which of the propositions most strongly engaged their own imaginations. I was somewhat surprised to see that each of the six propositions had advocates among the core team members, so they were enlisted to lead the design activity around "their" proposition at the session. I then briefly described the open space method that we would be using and their role as leaders in that process.[4]

Design and Destiny Session

The third and final session of the Appreciative Inquiry process at St. Agatha was held on Sunday, October 7, 2007.[5] The guiding theme for the day was articulated as: *Designing the future: What is the road that St. Agatha will walk with Christ? Discerning the invitation and call from God and making a personal and communal commitment to respond in faith.*

Again the day was beautiful and began with a well-attended and spirited celebration of Eucharist. There were about sixty-five people in attendance, a good number, but it did continue the slight dwindling in the number of participants over the three sessions. The liturgical readings for the day were especially fortuitous. The first reading from the book of the Prophet Habakkuk (1:2-3; 2:2-4) included: "Then the LORD answered me and said: / Write down the vision clearly upon the tablets, / so that one can read it readily. / For the vision still has its time, / presses on to fulfillment, and will not disappoint; / if it delays, wait for it, / it will surely come, it will not be late." The second reading from Paul's letter to Timothy (2 Tim 1:6-8, 13-14) was a reminder of the gift of the Spirit that God had given. The gospel passage from Luke (17:5-10) was the parable of the mustard seed, a parable to assure the apostles that they had adequate faith for the task at hand. In his preaching, Father Dowling effectively connected the Scriptures to the task of the afternoon session, continuing what he had written in the parish bulletin that day:

> The vision that we have as individuals, and the dream of St. Agatha that has emerged from the memories and dreams of over 100 parishioners that will be revealed today, are borne out of deep faith and the great hope that God will do great things for us if, as Paul says today to Timothy, we "stir into flames the gift of God that you have through the imposition of hands." That gift given us through the Holy Spirit is a spirit, not of cowardice, but a spirit of "power, love and self control." This, my friends, is the power of faith.

After lunch Dowling began the session by leading prayer according to the usual format. He had chosen as the scriptural text the Lucan pre-ascension story where Jesus promises to send his spirit to the apostles (Luke 24:36-49). He then revealed the dream of St. Agatha (appendix N), which had been printed on a three-by-four-foot sheet of paper and was draped over the front of the altar. He read the dream and the people applauded but, to my ears, their reaction was not overly enthusiastic. Why? Maybe because they needed some time to absorb the rather long and involved statement? Maybe it was simply recognized as the compilation of the statements that they had previously heard? The reception was fine, just not rousing.

Again, the pastor's reflection was left open for me to continue. I introduced the session by recalling the work of the first two sessions and the preparation that the core team did to prepare for this session. I then told them a story of the building of one of the great cathedrals of Europe. The story is about a new bishop who goes to review the work of a nearly complete (after decades of work) cathedral. He asks various workmen what they are doing and gets a detailed description of the task being performed. Carpenters report on how they are constructing some pews. Stonecutters describe how they are assembling the grand altar. He then asks a woman sweeping in the sacristy what she is doing and she stands tall in pride and replies, "Your Excellency, I'm building a cathedral." I told the story as a way of encouraging them to always hold the vision before them and to see the value in every step that needs to be taken. I emphasized that the dream destination is reached step-by-step, that we do what is possible today and tomorrow new possibilities are revealed. While the dream is before us, our faithfulness is revealed in the taking of individual steps.

Open Space Design Group Work

I introduced the work of the session by explaining the possibility propositions and how we would be using them in a modified open space method. A basic principle of the method is to allow participants to select the area of their involvement. This allows the participants to bring their passion to the work as a means of encouraging the acceptance of responsibility for action. I described our "passion" as the gift that God has given each of us. Some are going to be passionate about how we worship. Others may care more about how we can grow the parish. Both areas are a part of the dream, and God has given this parish (through the participants) the gifts that it needs to realize the vision. The open space process was to give them a chance to bring their gifts to the service of realizing the vision. By way of instruction, I promised them that they didn't have to talk about anything unless it truly interested them and that they would have complete control over any action or work with which they would be involved going forward. To that end, I said that this was a time to be practical. As they were discussing the possibility propositions, they were to make suggestions that they had the authority to decide and that they were willing to accept the responsibility to implement. Therefore, this was not a time to say, "The parish council should do . . ." Rather, this was a time to think, "*I* will do [what], by [when]."

Of course, the person must act within the scope of their authority or position within the community. For example, at St. Agatha, in the designing of a program of evangelization, no one person had the authority to say that St. Agatha would adopt a particular program of evangelization. They might say, however, "I am willing to volunteer to help in a program of evangelization"; or, "I will contact the archdiocese to determine what resources are available for developing a program of evangelization." Or even, several persons might say that they are going to approach the pastor and the parish council and ask to be appointed as the parish evangelization committee, which will develop a proposal for parish consideration. Those statements are within the scope of their position within the community and when combined with the commitment of others, helps St. Agatha live their evangelization element of their dream into reality.

With the process described, the core team member who was designated to lead the design process for each possibility proposition (as determined at the core team meeting) came forward and read the proposition. All those present were encouraged to listen to the reading of all the possibility propositions and decide which proposition they most cared about and would work on. After they were all read, I answered questions to clarify the process and the scope of each proposition. This assisted people as they decided where their passion would best find expression. I let people know that they could move between the groups if they had multiple interests. According to Harrison Owen, the one law of open space technology is the law of two feet.[6] Simply, the law of two feet says that anytime that you don't think that you are learning or contributing to the group that you are in, use your two feet and join a different group. At that, we broke down into six groups that went to designated areas of the assembly hall where their propositions had been posted. Additional sheets of newsprint and pens and report forms were also available for their use.

The process followed in the small groups proved to be very effective.[7] An important part of that process design was that the discussion concerning each element of the proposition began by appreciating the ways in which this element was already present in the parish. This appreciative approach was important because it helped ground the discussion in that which is most life-giving in the current reality. As such, each discussion was a small AI process that began with a Discovery phase.

While they worked, I circulated among the groups. They had a little over an hour to work. Periodically, I would give additional instructions to the groups like: If you have an idea that you think will advance the parish toward the dream but don't know if it fits into the group you are in, put out the idea anyway. Our goal is to generate as many ideas as possible, while remaining true to the vision we have created.

There seemed to be great energy and interaction in the groups. People were clearly engaged, which became evident in the reports of their work. The reports were written on the forms provided, which was to aid the core team in the management task to follow.

After a short break we had the leaders report, giving all the detail they could. Every group had surfaced multiple ideas and had begun to act on them. Almost every idea had accountability assigned. People seemed "wowed" by some of the reports and the ideas that surfaced. Some ideas received spontaneous support and affirmation. I was amazed by the breadth of ideas and the creativity. Many practical and doable ideas were presented.[8]

After each report I had the Design team stand and be recognized and there seemed to be genuine appreciation of the reports and the ideas that were being presented. I closed the reporting with some observations that affirmed the work the parish had done through this process. I noted the energy and excitement that was present. I affirmed the principles of Appreciative Inquiry as a way of continuing to move forward and especially encouraged that the parish keep the positive image of the vision always before them. I stated my respect for what they had done and that they had a great dream, which I believed they would live their way into. In fact, through the process they had already realized parts of their dream. These comments were affirmed by many who nodded their agreement.

Father Dowling then began the closing of the session by stating his pride in the parish and his appreciation for all that they had done. He affirmed the core team and had them recognized. He then led the community in a closing ritual.

The closing prayer service was designed to ritually invite the people to "sign on" to the dream, making a commitment to help St. Agatha live her dream into reality. The printed three-by-four-foot sheet with the dream was placed on the altar, and he had everyone come forward to the altar and sign the dream. They then remained gathered around the altar. Then we joined hands and prayed in a circle and sang along to a recording of "Grateful" by Hezekiah Walker. It was obviously an emotional moment for many and it seemed a fitting way to end the process.

Core Team Follow-Up

The core team met the Tuesday after the final session and we began by appreciating the session on Sunday. I began by asking, "What did we do well and what did you most appreciate about the session?" There was enthusiasm as we discussed the open space method and they thought that the process had been clearly explained and facilitated. The team recognized that allowing people to select the Design group they would join was very important. This allowed people to connect their passion to the vision and was seen as the key to the success of the session. Many commented on the great amount of energy that was present in the process, and they were impressed by the steadfast commitment of people to the process. It was noted how the parishioners had taken ownership of the parish and were willing to accept responsibility. The process invited all the participants to offer their giftedness to the work of the parish, which resulted in many parishioners who previously were only involved through participation in worship activities to accept new responsibility and find ways to increase their level of participation in the life of the parish. The "learning" from the session was that people will accept responsibility for that which they care about.

I then asked, "What was affirming of the parish?" It was noted that the parish has a lot to build on, and they recognized the giftedness present in the parish. The interaction in the groups was open, and everyone's ideas were welcomed and respected. Specifically one person noted that no one said, "We tried that before and it didn't work." Another member made a very poignant observation that the process had broken down barriers and had allowed diverse opinions to be expressed. These diverse opinions were listened to with respect and taken seriously by her group. The core team valued that St. Agatha now has an organized plan for going forward. Stated in terms of the overall purpose of the process, we had created a road map for St. Agatha to walk in faith and move forward with Christ.

Having reviewed the previous parish session, the core team then engaged in a discussion about the overall process, which I will report on in the next chapter. But an important final task for the core team was to address organizational matters of implementing and continuing the work of the process. This final work had two areas of focus.

The first was to discuss how St. Agatha can continue the process that has begun. This discussion included practical issues of communication with parishioners who were not involved in the process and giving them a way to bring their gifts to the parish and participate in the fulfillment of the vision. An initial step in this was to have the signed dream statement presented to the full parish at the following Sunday liturgies. We discussed inviting those present at the Masses who had not been involved in the process to also commit to living the dream by "signing on." It would then be displayed in a prominent place in the assembly hall. The task of communicating the dream to inactive parishioners was given to the evangelization team.

The core team also put into place ways of monitoring the work plans developed in the proposition design groups. They decided that a new parish council structure was needed. In an amazing display of empowerment, they redesigned the parish council in about ten minutes, giving prominence to the six areas identified through the possibility propositions.

The second focus was to look at ways St. Agatha can continue to operate according to the principles of Appreciative Inquiry and continue to co-construct the life of the parish. We looked at some practical ways of always maintaining a positive focus by beginning every discussion in the parish with an inquiry into the life-giving forces, the blessings, that are present in the current situation. The hope is that St. Agatha has created a sustainable change in their organizational culture, which will allow them to be continually creative and faithful to the vision they have discerned through this process.

SECTION THREE

CHAPTER EIGHT

Restoring Communion through Appreciative Inquiry

In the previous chapters I told the story of the Appreciative Inquiry process at St. Agatha Catholic Church. After each of the three parish sessions, I met with the core team to discuss the previous parish session. In these discussions, the core team expressed their appreciation for the AI process and for the positive effect that it was having on the parish. As a process, it was clearly successful as a means of planning and articulating a vision for the future of the parish. This adds to the evidence that Appreciative Inquiry is valuable for organizational planning and development. But at St. Agatha our hope was not just to do some effective pastoral or strategic planning. Our hope was to assist the parish in restoring its sense of communion—to effect a reconciliation that would restore the parish community and to place behind it the events that had negatively impacted it. Were we successful?

To answer this question I want to give voice to those involved in the process. I recognize that these are subjective opinions. Perhaps it would have been possible to conduct a sociological study of the process, establish some behavioral or attitudinal criteria for "communion," and then measure for those criteria before and after, but that was not within the scope of my project with them. So, to give some indication of the effect of the Appreciative Inquiry process on the parish, I simply discussed it with the core team. This chapter will report on that discussion, using the questions I posed as discussion starters.

Reflections of the Core Team

As a prelude to this discussion, I told them that I wanted them to help me look at the before and after picture of St. Agatha. I said that my hope was to get a sense of what they thought and believed about the process and the effect of the process on the parish, that it was important that they simply tell me their truth and not try to "be nice to the facilitator" and tell me what they thought I would want to hear. The discussion was animated and all seemed both thoughtful and forthright in their replies.[1] Although my presence may have influenced their responses, I am reasonably confident that they tried to responded honestly, in part, because they wanted to share what they had learned from the process and to allow their wisdom to contribute to a reconciliation methodology others could use.

How would you compare St. Agatha before and after? What has been the effect of the process on the community of St. Agatha? How is St. Agatha different because of the work we have done?

The first core team member to respond identified herself as a former parishioner of Blessed Sacrament Church.[2] She said that before the process, the members of her former parish felt disconnected from St. Agatha, but now they feel connected. Everyone knows each other better. She said, "This was a new beginning for the parish and we were a part of defining that so now this is *our* parish." Another member of the core team that was from one of the closed parishes said it clearly: "A big change is that now people feel like this is their church."

Others echoed the theme of church ownership and involvement. Several spoke of the way the youth of the parish were given "voice" and how they used that voice to express a desire to be more integrally involved in the life of the church. Young adult participants in the process said they wanted more active participation in the life of the parish and the process gave them the opportunity to express that and to define that participation. As one person said, "Finally, young people were being asked to participate and they are excited to have the opportunity to make a contribution." Another spoke of the "former benchwarmers" saying that many parishioners who were previously "only come-to-Mass parishioners" were engaged throughout the process and have also made commitments to greater future participation.

In speaking of St. Agatha before, some noted that there was a lack of focus; "Now we are more focused and have a road map to go forward." Another added, "Before we were doing OK, but we were just maintaining. This process freed us up to move forward." A third team member said, "For a long time we were just going through the motions, waiting for the next shoe to drop, the next tragedy to be reported. We supported each other, but we didn't really know what to do about what was being revealed."

Finally, some spoke of the spiritual nature or foundation of the process, citing past efforts that failed. One said, "We tried town hall meetings in the past and they didn't work; nothing came from them. This time we had a spiritual focus; it was a kind of evangelization." Referring to the church motto of "Being Church after Church," another declared that the value of the process was that it helped them reclaim what it means to "Be Church *in* Church."

Can you tell me the effect the process had on the community of St. Agatha? Did it have an effect on how you feel about each other? Did it strengthen the bond you feel; do you feel closer? Are you more united? More like a family? Or is it pretty much the same?

In general, it was the opinion of the core team that the Appreciative Inquiry process did in fact promote a sense of unity and communion. It needs to be noted that the second topic that the core team chose for the process—We are one: united and strengthened in Christ—was specific to this concern. This topic selection indicates a desire for unity and the importance that the St. Agatha community places on their relationship with each other; it also demonstrates their belief that their relationship with each other is connected to their personal relationships with Christ. They viewed the process as facilitating the opportunity for them to claim ownership of the church. They recognized that through the process of creating a vision of the future, a common identity was established. That shared common identity, created within them a sense of community.

Again it was expressed that this was particularly true for those parishioners from the former cluster or closed parishes. "It brought reconciliation to the cluster churches that joined St. Agatha. We are now equal owners of St. Agatha." Another, seemingly speaking for all, put it quite succinctly, "We are one now."

I heard about St. Agatha because of all the publicity about Daniel McCormack's actions and the expressed desire for healing and the desire to move on. Has this process helped the parish to heal?

The short answer to this question was unanimously yes. Reflecting on the abuse allegations and the effect that it had on St. Agatha, one team member responded to what seemed to be an unspoken question: how could this have happened? He said that sometimes they felt like they had let the church down because they did not know the abuse was occurring and so did not protect the youth from a pastor they had trusted. He said that in large part it was because they had been kept passive; this was the pastor's church and no one even thought to challenge or question his actions. With the AI process at St. Agatha, now the people had a chance to step up and take responsibility and to be involved and claim their church. The implication is that now the people are better able to know what is going on and to protect the children. That sense of empowerment is a reflection of healing.

The process also seems to have helped the parish put the events of Daniel McCormack behind them. By that I mean his betrayal of trust and the effects of that on the parish no longer have the power to define the parish. Everyone still remembers the events and it will likely remain a part of the parish's self-understanding for a long time, but the event is no longer dominant in their self-awareness as a faith community. The process has seemed to help the parish to recognize and use their power to decide their own identity as they move forward together.

Do you know how this process has affected the youth who were abused and their families?

Most of the direct victims of the abuse and their families have severed their involvement in the parish and the school. Father Dowling continues to offer them pastoral care and individually encourages them to seek counseling or other services that might aid their own healing. One person expressed her discomfort with the amount of public information and discussion about the youth involved. She said that at some point the whole thing becomes voyeuristic and that the privacy of the youth needs to be respected so that they have control over where this is discussed. She felt it would be inappropriate for the parish to be having public discussions about the specifics of the abuse. "The process we did helped to make us a strong community that can nurture the victims. It is that way that we respond to them, not by public problem solving of the issue."

What effect did McCormack's action have on the parish and did this process have any impact in transforming that?

Someone offered this metaphor in response. "Before, with all that had gone on, we were like a closed up flower. There were good things here; we had blessings, but we were closed up. The process gave us a chance to bloom again." Another person expressed appreciation for the overall purpose that we had selected: Walking in Faith and Moving Forward with Christ. The purpose reflected the desire of the parishioners. No one is deny-ing anymore what McCormack had done or that it was awful. But the church *needed* to move past that to create a future. This theme continued to be expressed in response to the next question.

Some would say that you have to face the problem or hurt head on, that you need to talk about it and analyze what happened, redressing the wrong that was committed, etc. We didn't do that. This approach was from the other side. Do you think that it is OK that we didn't speak specifically about Daniel McCormack's betrayal of trust and its effect on the children and the community?

Again the core team was unified in their assertion that parish-ioners did not want to talk about McCormack and what he did. They noted that not once in the parish sessions did anyone seek to introduce that discussion. The time for that seemed to be past and "people seem to be healing." There was general agreement that to have made the sexual abuse of the children the focus of the process would have rendered the process ineffective. All agreed that it would have been very difficult to get the level of parish participation that we had if we had made that the focus. One person said gratefully, "This process moved us faster and quicker than trying to talk about what had happened." And another added, "We had lots of problems before (parish merg-ers/closings, McCormack, finances, etc.) and we were not really facing any of them. Now we faced all the problems, but we did it from the side of the solution. This was a paradigm shift and it helped us."

Noting that it was now about a year and a half since the allegations against Daniel McCormack had surfaced, I asked the core team about the timing of the process of St. Agatha? Could we or should we have done this sooner?

The group was *adamant* in saying that it would not have been possible to do the Appreciative Inquiry process much sooner than they did. The parish had needed some time for the emotions to settle and for Dowling to be in place as the pastor. Because there was an interim pastor for a year before Dowling was appointed, I asked the core team if he had been named pastor sooner, could they have done the process sooner? Again, they were adamant that they would have needed about this much time from the abuse allegation to be ready to decide to move forward.[3]

Other Reflections

While not responsive to particular questions posed, other reflections of the core team need to be noted.

There was a very spirited affirmation of the leadership of their pastor, Larry Dowling. Core team members (who are the lay leaders of the parish) declared that the AI process allowed his leadership to emerge, and it confirmed him as the pastor and parish leader who can help the church move forward. He was recognized as being affirming and inviting. His style of leadership, his spiritual depth, and his maturity and humility were all praised. One statement was widely affirmed: "You have given us solid, consistent, unbiased leadership." I find it interesting to note that it was in sharing his authority and leadership, that his leadership and authority as pastor were confirmed.

A religious sister on the core team observed that this process and the pastor's leadership approach reflected a shift in the operative ecclesiology of the parish. The church now has shared leadership. Previous leadership was very top-down (pastor controlled) and now the leadership is more participative and the church "ownership" is shared. There is a more participative and open ecclesiology being lived. Someone else said that it feels more democratic and now people are more respected and allowed to have responsibility and participation in decisions. To the core team, the AI process results and the process itself reflects a more desired ecclesiology.

Shortly after this core team meeting, this sister continued to reflect on leadership and ecclesiology in a follow-up communication. Reflecting on the two previous pastors with whom she had worked at St. Agatha, she noted that they probably would have welcomed the ecclesiological shift at St. Agatha that she witnessed through this process, but they lacked the necessary personal and leadership skills to make it happen. She thought that one former pastor would have lacked the patience to commit to such an extensive process. Another would speak the words of inclusivity, but in the end would not be able to relinquish control, which meant that the ideas and opinions of others were not honored. She wrote, "AI is great in that it gives a structure that could lead to something. . . . I think that AI is constructed on the assumption that people are willing and capable. So it naturally leads to a model of Church which is inclusive and empowering. The problem for 'the people' will always be that it all depends upon who is the pastor of our dear Church."[4]

One final reflection comes from a follow-up conversation with Dowling. He noted that he has reflected on this process and the effect it has had on St. Agatha in eucharistic terms. Observing that in the celebration of Eucharist, bread is blessed, broken, and given, he recognizes in Appreciative Inquiry's focus on the positive core a discovery or affirmation of the many ways that the parish and the people of the parish have been blessed. While the betrayal of trust of their former pastor has been a significant breaking of the community, the process has also given the members of the parish a way to bring the blessings that they have from God and give them as a gift to the community through a shared vision of the future.

The assessment of the core team of the Appreciative Inquiry process, while subjective, is emphatic. Yes, AI can be a strategy for reconciliation and it can lead to the restoration of communion in a faith community. Because reconciliation and a sense of communion are essentially private, internal perceptions, their reporting of those perceptions needs to be respected and valued.

CHAPTER NINE

Reconciliation and Communion Ecclesiology at St. Agatha Church

I share with the core team their assessment that the Appreciative Inquiry process at St. Agatha was a process of reconciliation and did lead to the restoration or strengthening of communion. I arrive at this conclusion through reflection on the events that I witnessed and experienced through the facilitation of the process.

Reconciliation Is, First and Foremost, Concerned with Relationships

The focus of the process at St. Agatha was on the relationships. This is most clearly seen in the topics selected. The first topic, *A vibrant and Spirit-filled church*, was expressive of the relationship that the church desired with God. It reflected the desire to be in "right relationship" with God and for the community of St. Agatha; this communal relationship with God found its expression in their Sunday celebration of Eucharist. The second topic, *We are one: united and strengthened in Christ*, can be read as a declaration of the community's desire for communion. It needs to be noted that while the desire is expressed for a united relationship among the members of the church, they recognize that the path to that unity is through their relationship with Christ. This expression of communion ecclesiology indicates the necessary interconnectedness of the horizontal and vertical relationships that are part of faithfulness for a church. The third topic, *Being church after church*, directed the focus of the process to an outward or missionary direction. This too is about right relationship: the right relationship of the church to the world or the context in which it is situated. The discussion of the parish around this topic was an expression of the desire of the parish, individually and communally, to represent Christ in their neighborhood.

Reconciliation Is Both a Goal and a Process

In the writings of Robert Schreiter and John Paul Lederach, there is agreement that reconciliation must be understood as being both a goal and a process. The theory and practice of Appreciative Inquiry also recognizes the importance of the process employed being an expression of the desired goal. More than just a theory and process of organizational development, AI is "a way of seeing and being in the world."[1] This is most clearly indicated in AI with the absolute "rule" to maintain the positive core as the focus in the process. AI purports that an organization will move toward that about which it most persistently inquires. If you have a positive goal, you must reflect that positive focus in the process employed. Likewise, AI would recognize that if reconciliation within the community is the goal, then the process to pursue that goal must reflect the community acting in a way that embodies a community that is already reconciled. The actions of the community must reflect the stated desire or goal. The AI process at St. Agatha had this type of integrity.

The purpose statement for the St. Agatha process was: *Walking in Faith and Moving Forward with Christ*. That is a statement of both goal and process. As a goal statement it expresses the desire to be faithful to Christ, both individually and communally. It also expresses as a goal the desire of the church to be reconciled and healed from the past events that have fractured their sense of unity and well being. More important, through the AI process at St. Agatha, the church was realizing the goal in deed. Through the process, they were acting in faith and they were collectively moving out of the painful events of the past that had created their need for reconciliation; they were becoming the reconciled community that they desired to be. In some ways, the goal was achieved in the decision to begin an Appreciative Inquiry process, and the process itself became the opportunity to define the particulars of that new identity and to learn and practice the patterns of behavior that would allow that new identity to be firmly established and sustainable as they continued to journey together as a community of faith.

Reconciliation Is Both Spirituality and Strategy

In the theological framework of a Christian spirituality of reconciliation, Robert Schreiter asserts the role of God as the primary agent of reconciliation. It follows therefore, that a ministry of reconciliation needs to be rooted in a spirituality, and Schreiter cautions a would-be minister of reconciliation from being too confident or dependent on strategies to bring about reconciliation. This is not to deny the need or place of strategies in a praxis of reconciliation, but to assert that reconciliation depends on God, even as God works through human action.

Appreciative Inquiry asserts a different perspective. While AI theory speaks infrequently about the goal of reconciliation within an organization, it is a very confident strategy. AI theory would recognize a church as being a "social construction," and as such, its identity and functioning is within the scope of the participants to create and define. AI theory would say: If a church wants to be reconciled, the church can create that reality. In AI theory, reconciliation would be, however, a sociological, not theological concept.

Appreciative Inquiry theory springs from the secular concern of organizational dynamics. While some authors[2] have written of the compatibility of AI to Christian theology and a reading of the Scriptures, in my reading of the AI literature, I found no stated position on religion or theological and spiritual belief systems. It can only be projected that AI would look only at "church" in social and human terms. That said, I think that in the use of AI within an ecclesial setting, the religious beliefs of the participants are respected. Pertinent to the process at St. Agatha, while AI theory would not assert that the church "should" reflect Gospel values, it would assert the ability of the participants in the process to create a church that reflects Gospel values, if that is the goal or the desire of participants. In one sense, while the theory of Appreciative Inquiry is theologically silent, it does allow the participants to act on their beliefs, and the theory resonates with a theology that views the world as a place of grace.

In that sense, while not containing overt statements of theology, an Appreciative Inquiry process can be an inherently spiritual activity. This was demonstrated in the process at St. Agatha. From the beginning conversations with the core team, the concerns expressed and the motivation for going forward were essentially spiritual. St. Agatha was a church wanting to be faithful, a faithfulness that needed to be expressed in their relationship to God, one another, and others. This spirituality not only was expressed with the use of religious imagery and action (ritual and prayer) but also was an expression of the spirituality of communion articulated by John Paul II in *Novo Millennio Ineunte*. The AI process encouraged and provided the opportunity for the parishioners of St. Agatha to demonstrate a great concern for one another. This was beyond an emotional concern for one another. Rather, it reflected an understanding of self that was in solidarity with others as part of one body, one church. They were hospitable and open to one another throughout the process as people who held each other in genuine respect. In their positive regard of one another, there was an assumption of the giftedness of all and that all had a place within the church. In this too, the AI process reflected the goal of restoring a church to communion, because it provided the structure and framework for the participants to act like a community. The AI process is dependent on the participants working together with openness and respect to achieve a mission or task, and the process reinforces that perspective by teaching the skills that can become a sustainable way of maintaining the relationship in the future. For this reason, AI has a strong tendency to contribute to the building of community.

Both Schreiter and Lederach situate the praxis of reconciliation within the church; within a community of faith. Specific to the writings of Schreiter, the AI process at St. Agatha created a place of safety, memory, and hope. The meetings of the core team and the three sessions of the parish were filled with honest and respectful dialogue. A spirituality of dialogue was very evident. People felt the safety to speak from their hearts and to express their dreams for their church. Together they recalled the best of their past and shared those memories as a means of laying the foundation for building their future together. Together, they created a community of hope in which the negative events of the past lost their hold on defining the identity and future of the community. While AI theory is not presented in the literature as a spiritual exercise, in fact, the engagement of the theory at St. Agatha was a decidedly spiritual strategy for effecting communion and building a community of faith.

Reconciliation Is a New Creation

Another aspect of the theological understanding of reconciliation, as presented by Schreiter, is that reconciliation is not the restoration of the previous situation or relationships; rather it results in a new creation. The core team for the AI process at St. Agatha were in universal agreement that the process had resulted in St. Agatha being a new creation. What exactly was that new creation?

Perhaps the most significant effect of the AI process at St. Agatha was that the operative ecclesiology of the parish shifted. In the previous model, the church was marked by a hierarchical leadership in which all considered the "owner" of the church to be the pastor. This created a closed system in which the parishioners were relegated to a passive role. A further characteristic was that there was little dialogue and communication about the concerns and issues that were present. The evidence of this is seen in the reports of the members from the closed parishes who never felt integrated into the life of St. Agatha. It also created the situation where the questionable actions of a pastor (e.g., unsupervised activity with minors) would not be questioned.

Through the AI process, a new type of parish has been given birth. As members of the core team claimed, the church now belongs to them. They gratefully credit the participative leadership style of their new pastor with making this possible. Today, they willingly accept the responsibility for shared leadership and for the parish as a whole. This shift in ecclesiology can be understood within the framework of communion ecclesiology.

As a foundation for his discussion of the various versions of communion ecclesiology and his attempt to create a synthesis of those versions that can be a unifying vision for the church, Dennis Doyle cited four elements that seem to always be present. Of these four elements, three are illustrated in the "new" St. Agatha Church.[3]

The first is that there is a clear emphasis on the spiritual relationships present, over the more juridical or institutional aspects of the church. While the parishioners at St. Agatha Church recognize and, for the most part, value that they are part of a larger body, the Roman Catholic Church, their expressed concern was for the more immediate parochial relationships. They are concerned about their personal relationships with God and how they worship God together. They are concerned about how they can be faithful together in their life as a parish. The evidence for this is seen in the defined purpose of the process, the topic selection and the resulting sense of communion that they now experience.

The second element of a communion ecclesiology present in St. Agatha's new model of church is the importance that they place on the celebration of Eucharist as a sign of their communion. It is important to note that the celebration of Eucharist was a part, at least indirectly, of the AI process. Clearly, there is nothing in AI theory or practice that includes the celebration of Eucharist, but each of the three parish gatherings followed the pattern of beginning with the celebration of Eucharist at ten thirty, followed by a meal and the session with the 4-D process activity. The celebration of Eucharist was connected to the afternoon AI activity through the preaching during the celebration and the prayer of the faithful. Sometimes we were able to further link the Eucharist to the AI activity by making reference to the Mass readings of the day during the afternoon session. It is impossible to determine the effect of the celebration of Eucharist on the results of the AI process at St. Agatha, but it does indicate the central importance the celebration of Eucharist has in the identity of the St. Agatha faith community and is a sign of communion ecclesiology being operative.

Finally, Doyle highlights that within communion ecclesiology, there is a dynamic interplay between unity and diversity. This also is visible at St. Agatha. The AI process helped create this identity at St. Agatha in that a guiding principle of Appreciative Inquiry is to create the broadest possible participation and to foster the creation of a unifying vision that can hold the input from diverse participation.

St. Agatha has become a model of a Vatican II parish and an example of communion ecclesiology in that there is broad, active participation of the laity who are empowered to assume their responsibilities within the church community. They are very much a eucharistic community since their celebration of Eucharist and their lives together reflect both the vertical and horizontal dimensions of communion.

Perhaps the clearest indication that the AI process facilitated a reconciliation that led to a "new" St. Agatha is found in the dream narrative of the parish. The importance of narratives is recognized in both Appreciative Inquiry theory and in the Christian understanding of reconciliation that is represented in the writings of Schreiter.

Schreiter points to narratives as being important articulations of identity. The stories we tell about ourselves reflect the truth that we believe about ourselves and who we are. Developing this idea, Schreiter writes of violence as being narratives of the lie. That is, when our humanity is damaged through violence, it creates the untruthful "story" that our lives are somehow less than the humanity that the Creator intended for us. A sign of reconciliation is when the victim is able to confront the narrative of the lie with a new narrative that reaffirms their humanity. That sign is present at St. Agatha. They have reaffirmed their identity as a faithful community and, while they have not forgotten the memory of their former pastor's betrayal of their trust or the closing of their parishes, those memories have now been resituated and those stories no longer have the toxic power to define their identity.

Appreciative Inquiry theory supports the importance of narratives and goes one step further in saying that our narratives actually create the reality of who we are. Every organization has an inner dialogue and the organization change theory of AI is that for change to occur, it is necessary to change the inner dialogue of the organization. That is what the AI process at St. Agatha did, and it led to the creation of their dream statement as an articulation of the desired future of the parish. But more than a statement of the desired future, it is also an articulation of their present identity, in that the process put into place the actions that will allow the parish to live that dream into reality. It is in this aspect that the dream statement is an articulation of St. Agatha as a "new creation" and gives further credence to the claim that AI can be an effective strategy for effecting reconciliation.

Appreciative Inquiry in the Praxis of Reconciliation

My involvement in the AI process at St. Agatha was as an agent of reconciliation. Throughout my facilitation of the process, reconciliation was my concern, although I only infrequently stated that concern. In my work with the core team and in the initial session with the broader parish, my concern for reconciliation was declared. In the actual Appreciative Inquiry sessions, however, we very seldom spoke of reconciliation. We never identified and articulated the need for reconciliation. We never asked during the process, "Is this moving us toward reconciliation?" The project was to engage the parish in a discussion of their future, guided by the theory and practice of AI, and to see if "what happens" can rightly be understood as reconciliation. As I have written above, I think the project has demonstrated that AI can be an effective strategy for effecting reconciliation within a church community. Now I want to explore the implications of that discovery for the praxis of reconciliation.

I viewed my role in the process as one of consultant and facilitator. In my work with the core team I was responsible for sharing a knowledge of Appreciative Inquiry and assisting them in the definition of a process that would be consistent with AI practice. Along with leading the definition of the process, I was responsible for sharing in the leadership and facilitation of the process.

Schreiter uses the postresurrection stories in the gospels to identify a four-step process in the reconciliation ministry of Jesus: accompaniment, hospitality, reconnecting, and commissioning. He asserts that the first two steps are skills that can be developed and employed by a minister of reconciliation while the latter two are dependent on the gratuity of God. Within the AI process, facilitation can be understood as compatible with the activities of accompaniment and hospitality. I initiated a relationship with the parish in which I was willing to be with them in the situation created by the removal of their former pastor. In my role of facilitator, I accompanied them in the process that followed. Schreiter defined hospitality as the creation of a safe place of trust where human communication is possible again. At the center of the AI process is dialogue and communication, where all have been empowered and given voice. In the process at St. Agatha we created the space for that dialogue. The process at St. Agatha also resulted in a reconnection of the people with each other and a renewed acceptance of the mission

that they have as a church. Within Schreiter's ministerial framework and the Christian understanding of reconciliation, this is
recognized and welcomed as the work of God. Within the secular
theory of Appreciative Inquiry, this is seen as the organization
constructing that connectedness and sense of purpose through
the dialogue facilitated within the process. This is a significant
difference and it has implications for praxis.

Within the framework of a Christian spirituality of reconciliation, while an agent of reconciliation can find motivation for
ministry in the vocation to be an ambassador of Christ and to
continue the work of Christ in the world, this framework suggests an acceptance of a certain impotency to enact that reconciliation in favor of accepting a dependency on God to provide
the reconciliation desired. Ultimately, Schreiter writes that a
minister of reconciliation find solace in a spirituality that
includes a belief in the eschatological promise of reconciliation
while continuing to work for reconciliation in this world. We
can employ strategies and seek to be effective, but ultimately
we are dependent on God to provide "success." The Appreciative Inquiry framework holds out the promise that all things,
including reconciliation and peace, are possible in this world
and that such a reconciled reality can be constructed through
the creative design of strategies and applications of the principles of AI. While significantly different, I am not convinced
that these two methodological frameworks are contradictory.

To hold these two divergent approaches together in a praxis
of reconciliation, it is necessary to recognize that in the praxis
of reconciliation there are two fields of concern—personal and
social. In every situation of conflict, both aspects need consideration. On the personal level, the need for reconciliation is often
expressed as a need for healing that can make forgiveness possible. On the social level, reconciliation is about the need to create
a social system or structure where justice is protected and the
conflict will not recur. As Schreiter has observed, and as my own
experience confirms, there is no strategy that provides that
personal healing. While we can accompany the victim pastorally

and therapeutically, for personal healing that can lead to their ability to forgive another, for the personal healing that can lead to a desire to restore right relationship, we are clearly dependent on God. And without the desire of the affected individuals to restore the relationship, it is not possible to address a conflict and to construct a peace. Once a measure of personal healing has occurred, however, and there is a desire to construct a new relationship, then the social constructionism principle of Appreciative Inquiry would assert that such a peace can be constructed by the parties involved. As a secular theory, AI is silent as to the role (if any) of God in that work.

I don't think that precludes AI from being employed as a strategy for reconciliation. Nor does it preclude the process itself from being adapted for use in an ecclesial context or prevent those who employ the strategy from articulating their motivation for the work in religious terms. Nor would it prevent one from believing that it is God who is effecting the new creation, working through the parties involved in the conflict to construct a peace. Accepting the social construction principle of Appreciative Inquiry is not to deny the role of God in the reconciliation process any more than accepting a scientific theory of evolution denies the role of God as creator.

Understanding and Responding to Conflict

A key underlying concern in the praxis of reconciliation is how to understand and respond to conflict. In this, Appreciative Inquiry offers a significantly different view and methodology than expressed in the writing of Schreiter and Lederach.

Lederach writes (and Schreiter would agree) that conflict presents an opportunity for transformation. Reconciliation requires more than the resolution of the conflict; it requires that one look to the web of relationships that are affected by the conflict, address the causes of the conflict, and create a social structure where those causes are no longer present.

The methodology is to move toward the conflict and to address the conflict directly. To do that, it is necessary for a setting to be created where it is safe for the parties to tell their story, to tell their "truth" concerning the situation or conflict. Lederach would see the sharing of narratives as an opportunity to analyze the causes of the conflict and to engage the moral imagination to envision a way to peace. Schreiter would suggest that it is necessary to remain with the parties in conflict, with a preference for being present to the victim, allowing them to tell the narrative of the conflict until, through the grace of God, the story begins to shift and loose its hold on determining the future of the one who has been victimized. Schreiter's emphasis would be to accompany the victim in the conflict; Lederach's emphasis would be to facilitate the dialogue between the parties in conflict and to try to imagine a way through the conflict to a better, more peaceful situation. While both would address the conflict as an opportunity to reconcile relationships and not just to solve a problem, the focus on conflict is the same as in a problem-solving strategy.

The approach of Appreciative Inquiry is 180 degrees different. Instead of moving toward the conflict, this theory would suggest that the conflict be bracketed and set aside in favor of a different focus—the positive core. Here the approach is to remember and to celebrate the best of the past and the more life-giving aspects of the organization. Then the creativity and the imagination of the group is stimulated to come to a dream (expressed through narratives) in which that positive core is further enhanced. Building on the passion and interest of the participants, implementation of the dream is simultaneous with the process as the organization begins to act on its dream and to create a new and improved organization. Conflict is addressed only indirectly, in that the focus is on the construction of a social situation in which the conflict is no longer present.

Appreciative Inquiry's distinct approach to conflict is important in that it offers a radically different methodology to the praxis of reconciliation and, as such, broadens the possible approaches available to a minister of reconciliation in that work.

While distinctive from the praxis considerations of Schreiter and Lederach, it is not completely foreign to a praxis of reconciliation. I find it reminiscent of the peace process used by the Truth and Reconciliation Commission in South Africa. There the decision was made to grant amnesty to all parties willing to speak the truth about their role in the atrocities committed during the time of apartheid rule. It was decided that the granting of amnesty was needed to make possible the constructing of a new South Africa, because to attempt to respond to the past violence through a judicial process would exhaust the resources of the country and would prevent the country from moving forward. There the conflict was not denied and it was the focus of many public hearings, but the specific injustices were not directly addressed in favor of allowing the country to move forward and to direct their efforts in constructing a postapartheid reality. Amnesty created the needed space for the activity of social constructionism.[4]

There are some commonalities between the approach of dealing with conflict directly, proposed by Schreiter and Lederach, and the approach of Appreciative Inquiry, which directs the activity toward a desired solution. Both place a priority on dialogue and respectful communication and encourage the telling of narratives as a part of that communication. Both would be based in the theory of social constructionism, although the methodology for that activity is only concretely developed in the Appreciative Inquiry framework. Both seek to engage the imagination of the participants.

It is in this area, the engagement of imagination, that the Appreciative Inquiry process can make another important contribution. Lederach has written on the importance of a moral imagination in the work of reconciliation. His writing includes a concern for how to develop such an imagination, but his writing is less clear about how to foster the engagement of the imagination in the praxis of reconciliation. AI offers a framework for such an engagement of the imagination. Specifically, the disciplines that Lederach writes about are capable of stimulating the development of the imagination; the AI process encourages that all suspend judgment in favor of being curious about the ideas of others. AI creates space for the creative act to emerge through the 4-D process. This is seen especially in the dream imagery exercises and the creative report presentations of those dreams. And finally, AI provides a process in which the acceptance of risk is tolerable because the changes being acted on are directly tied to the concerns and dreams of the ones assuming the risk.

I think that my work with St. Agatha parish can rightly be understood as a ministry of reconciliation. Jean-Marie Tillard wrote that "Communion is not the same as a gathering together of friends. . . . It is the coming together in Christ of men and women who have been reconciled."[5] The faith community at St. Agatha meets that criteria for communion. Appreciative Inquiry can be an effective strategy for reconciliation in an ecclesial setting and can help restore communion in a church that has suffered a disruption to that communion.

I think Appreciative Inquiry theory is a valuable dialogue partner in the development of a practical theology of reconciliation, and the AI process has a place in the praxis of reconciliation. In the final chapter, I will seek to situate Appreciative Inquiry within that praxis and offer some considerations that need further exploration.

The Place of Appreciative Inquiry in the Praxis of Reconciliation

Appreciative Inquiry is a useful strategy for effecting reconciliation and helping to restore communion in ecclesial communities. While AI theory has its roots in the secular discipline of organizational dynamics and much of the practice of AI has evolved through its use by organizational development consultants with businesses and other secular institutions, I used it effectively at St. Agatha Catholic Church to assist that faith community respond to the effects of traumatic events within the community.

Appreciative Inquiry does have a place in the praxis of reconciliation, but what is that place? Are there times and situations in which AI will be a more or less appropriate approach for a minister of reconciliation to employ? I turn to those questions in this final chapter. Again reflecting on the experience at St. Agatha, I will offer some observations and reflections that will begin to situate AI within a praxis of reconciliation for ecclesial settings. In this I include some of the limitations that I see and questions that remain for possible further investigation.

Required Mindset to Use AI Effectively for Reconciliation

Perhaps it needs to be said: there can be no reconciliation if those in conflict do not have a genuine desire for reconciliation. There is no strategy for force-feeding reconciliation. Even in situations where people are not able to imagine reconciliation but genuinely desire reconciliation, some progress toward that is often possible. But without the sincere desire, it is not possible.

Recently, the staff of the Precious Blood Ministry of Reconciliation was invited into a parish that was under considerable duress. A new pastor had terminated the employment of a popular long-term staff member. That action and the response of angry parishioners had created a very acrimonious situation. Some in the parish perceived the termination as an injustice that they needed to rectify. Our initial work was with this group of parishioners. Their motivation was a faithful concern for justice. Justice was their key value. They spoke of the desire for reconciliation; however, their understanding of reconciliation was the enforcement of justice. They were not able to consider the possibility of restoring right relationship with their pastor; they simply insisted that he be removed. They could envision no other possibility. They were not able (at that time) to desire the restoration of communion; they wanted someone excommunicated. Reconciliation was simply not possible.

Helping to create the desire for reconciliation is an important ministerial concern and may be considered a first step in a praxis of reconciliation. For this ministry, Robert Schreiter lays the necessary foundation in his assertion that a first step is to accompany the victims, creating the space where victims can tell the story of the harm done to them. Many methodologies can be employed to assist individuals and groups to dialogue and share these narratives. In our ministry of reconciliation in Chicago, we have acquired a strong appreciation for the use of Peacemaking Circles.[1] In this practice, a ritualized process of communication is used to create the sacred space needed for individuals to speak of the trauma that has affected them. In cases of severe trauma, individual therapy is often needed to help an individual experience the personal healing necessary before they desire reconciliation.

Accepting a New Paradigm

The use of an Appreciative Inquiry process requires that the participants accept, at least implicitly, the underlying assumptions and principles of the theory. The process of discovering the positive core and using that as the foundation for dreaming and designing a new reality is dependent on a particular understanding of the nature of organizations and the process of change. If the participants are skeptical of the theory, there must at least be a willingness to allow the underlying principles and assumption to guide the activity. It is a new way of thinking and it is not always an easy shift in thinking for people to make. In my conversations with peers during this project, I heard repeatedly, "What do you mean, you aren't talking about the problems? You cannot hope to effect reconciliation by denying the problems." While various strategies or methodologies may be employed, currently the praxis of reconciliation has an orientation to focus and deal directly with the conflict. Appreciative Inquiry cannot be used unless the participants can shift away from that more traditional understanding and embrace a new approach.

When the situation and the wounds that cause the conflict are recent, it may not be possible or appropriate to suggest that the victims put aside their story of injury and harm in favor of the necessary shift of focus required by the AI method.

Requirements of Leadership

Within a church or organization that desires reconciliation, leadership is key. Specifically, the manner in which authority and leadership are exercised are important indicators as to the possibility of engaging the organization in an AI process. The AI process is dependent on broad participation and the creation of a forum where all are empowered to express their views. This was very clearly demonstrated at St. Agatha. The willingness of the pastor to largely forego control and to allow the process to unfold was a key factor in its success. In the language of John Paul Lederach, the pastor had the needed moral imagination. In accepting the risk of allowing the process to unfold, the pastor did not abdicate his responsibility of leadership; nor did anyone forget that he was the duly appointed pastor. While there were some implicit parameters that guided the dreaming of the participants, the pastor was able to accept the risk of not controlling the specific outcome of the process.

For a pastor who has already embraced a collaborative model of leadership, the required broad participation of the parishioners and the sharing of decision making found in an AI process will not be threatening. In fact, it will be embraced as providing a needed structure for inviting that participation and soliciting the commitment of all to "own" their parish.

Beyond the goal of effecting reconciliation, employing an AI process teaches the behaviors of open, respectful dialogue, the acceptance and sharing of responsibility, and the empowerment of the laity for mission, all hallmarks of the communion ecclesiology that flows from Vatican II. Because the process is concerned with sustainable change, it is hoped that the process does not end but teaches a way of being in relationship with one another that can be an important element of their common life. The AI process at St. Agatha was a church affirming its desire to be in right relationship with each other and practicing the skills that build community.

The attitude of those in leadership positions is critical. An AI process will result in a changed organization or church. Part of that change may be the emergence of a model of shared authority in leadership. Those in leadership positions must be ready to participate in the construction of that new reality, and they must be ready to welcome the change.

Commitment to the Work of a Process

Throughout the process with St. Agatha, I was concerned about the demand the process was placing on the time constraints of the participants. Simply, the process was a lot of work and required a significant commitment of time. There were four meetings with the pastor and parish leadership to explain Appreciative Inquiry theory and to get to a commitment to do the process. In all, the core team met ten times, usually for two hours. The three parish sessions were from ten thirty in the morning to four o'clock in the afternoon. There was much work done outside of the formal meetings. That is a large time commitment to ask members of a parish. An AI process is not a quick fix and before beginning the process, a community must be prepared to make a significant commitment of time and effort. That said, in my ministry I am continuing to investigate if a less comprehensive approach is beneficial for a community that desires reconciliation. Can a session for one afternoon be designed that is beneficial for the community in conflict? Can AI theory be incorporated into a four-evening parish mission or a six-week Lenten series in a way that helps to restore or strengthen the sense of communion in a church?

The Place of Appreciative Inquiry in the Praxis of Reconciliation

While I think that Appreciative Inquiry can be an effective strategy for the restoration of communion in an ecclesial setting, it is best understood as one method or strategy among many that may be employed in the ministry. It is an addition to the praxis, not a replacement. For that reason, it is necessary to think of the AI process in relation to the other elements within the praxis. This is true in regard to three interrelated aspects: timing, its use with other strategies, and the context in which an application of an AI process may be more or less appropriate.

Appreciative Inquiry does not seem to be a first strategy in responding to conflict. The core team at St. Agatha was most adamant that their process would not have been possible much sooner than it occurred. They said that the parish had needed some time to allow the emotions to be expressed and to settle down and process the events of the past before they could be ready to think about creating a new future. The shock of the accusation against their pastor and his removal from the church occurred about eighteen months before the initial parish session. Although that was the precipitating event, in fact, the disruption in the life of the parish continued from that time until the AI process began. During the process Definition phase, McCormack pleaded guilty to criminal charges; there was a related but secondary issue with the principal; the week before the process began, a victims' advocacy group protested at St. Agatha because of the presence of Cardinal George. So the event that disturbed the sense of communion of the parish was not over, but the emotional "heat" of the issue had subsided and some of the core team members described that as being a measure of healing. How did that healing occur?

I did not ask for a detailed narrative of the events that led to that healing and it predated my involvement in the parish, but generally what was described was a process of accompaniment. This accompaniment was twofold: the community being present to each other in their talking about the events and seeking to be a source of support to one another, and the accompaniment of new pastoral leadership. When looked at through the lens of Schreiter's praxis, this is an example of how accompaniment and hospitality can create a community of safety, memory, and hope and make the space for the grace of God to be experienced. The victims came to experience the healing grace of God in the telling of their narratives; a grace that allows the memory of the betrayal of trust to be resituated, because it no longer had the power to determine the identity or future of the community. With that measure of healing, primarily effected through the accompaniment and the hospitality of having a safe place to remember and relate the narrative of the betrayal, the community was now ready to allow a new creation to emerge. Until this measure of personal healing had been experienced, the core team did not think that an AI process would be possible.

The significance of this is that, for the community at St. Agatha, the initial work of reconciliation was in keeping with the praxis suggestions of Schreiter and Lederach, since there was a need to have a safe place to look at the conflict or traumatic events directly and honestly, to articulate the effects of that on their lives, and to have the time for the grace of God to be revealed.

As stated in the previous chapter, AI is a theory of organizational dynamics and is concerned with the social construction of an organizational identity and fulfillment of its mission or purpose. While it is possible to speculate about how the principles of AI might be applied to our understanding of persons, AI theory did not develop out of a desire or concern for effecting personal transformation or healing. The primary focus is not personal but social. It is in this that the place of AI in the praxis of reconciliation is revealed.

The primary value of AI to the praxis is that it offers a concrete and effective method that facilitates sustainable organization transformation through social construction. One of the elements of a Christian understanding of reconciliation proposed by Schreiter is that it results in a new creation. The praxis is unclear, however, in providing concrete direction on how to facilitate that construction. Appreciative Inquiry fills that void in the praxis.

At St. Agatha, the community was ready to move forward into a new reality. The participants individually had come to a point where they were willing to set aside the events of the betrayal of trust perpetrated by Daniel McCormack and to begin anew. They desired a restoration of right relationship as a community. Appreciative Inquiry theory provided the method to achieve that desired reconciliation. It created a forum to change the inner dialogue as a church and to establish a new identity. It provided the method to define a vision and mission for the future and to design a way to achieve that mission. Communion was effected through the shared commitment of the participants to that vision and mission.

When I think about the need for reconciliation within the church, I believe that there are many situations where AI theory and practice may be helpful. In the introduction to this book, I wrote that not only is there a widespread recognition of the need for reconciliation in the church, there is an equally broad desire among the pastoral leaders of the church to effect that reconciliation. The desire to be a church in communion is very evident. Seldom is there a need to create that desire, but often there is a sense of helplessness and impotency among pastoral leaders as to how to respond to the polarization that is present and to effect that desired reconciliation, how to construct a church in communion. For them, I believe AI offers a practical way of responding.

In particular, AI can be helpful in the building of community through the creation of a shared identity found in a shared vision and mission for the future. This is an important pastoral concern in the consolidation of parishes or other church ministries. I believe that it can be helpful for the integration of multicultural faith communities through the fostering of respectful dialogue and the bringing together of diverse concerns and dreams. I have used AI process to assist religious congregations to dialogue and find the common vision needed for defining their mission in the world. Appreciative Inquiry is capable of addressing complex, multiple-party social situations. While less certain, I also believe that it can help a community that is fractured along theological or ideological lines because of its focus on the positive core and the discovery of the shared life-giving aspects already present in the life of the community. I think there are many possibilities for the use of AI in a praxis of reconciliation within the church that need to be explored and tested, which I hope to do in my continuing ministry of reconciliation.

Appreciative Discernment

While Appreciative Inquiry theory and practice has its roots in a secular discipline, it is possible to think of it as a spiritual activity that is easily incorporated into the spiritual life of the community. As described in the previous chapter, the AI process at St. Agatha was essentially an exercise that reflected a spirituality of communion.

In some of the initial meetings with the leadership of St. Agatha, I "baptized" AI theory and christened it "Appreciative Discernment."[2] This was part of a successful effort to make the theory accessible to them by speaking of the theory in language familiar to church people. It was a way of representing the AI process as a spiritual activity; a way for a church to be faithful.

After those initial discussions, I essentially abandoned the use of the phrase "Appreciative Discernment" in favor speaking of the process in secular language. This project was my first attempt at facilitating a "full-blown" AI process. In large part, my decision to employ secular language was motivated by my desire to be carefully faithful to the principles of AI. While the decision to employ the secular language may have been appropriate in the research project that I described, in my ministry today I make full use of our religious vocabulary.

In working in ecclesial settings, I acknowledge the secular roots, but I refer to AI as the spiritual activity of Appreciative Discernment. The concept of Appreciative Discernment needs further development. Part of that may be to articulate the place of prayer and rituals within the process. That was a part of the process at St. Agatha, but I think that further possibilities need to be explored. Some questions or examples: How could the participants be encouraged to include the ongoing process in their private prayer life? Is there a place for the communal celebration of the sacrament of penance when using AI as part of a praxis of reconciliation? If the celebration of Eucharist is a part of the process (as it was at St. Agatha), are there ways to highlight that sacrament as a sacrament of reconciliation? These are questions that I now explore and hope others in the ministry will also consider and will share the results of their experimentation.

There is a need for reconciliation within the church. It is hard to find a church community that does not need to pay attention to fostering and strengthening their communion with one another. In some ways, that is part of the journey of a pilgrim people being called toward the vision of the church as the Body of Christ. And in times of polarizing conflict, the church requires that pastoral leaders be ambassadors of Christ, effecting the needed reconciliation through thoughtful and pastoral intervention. The theory and practice of Appreciative Inquiry can be just such an intervention, and it is an effective and needed component in a praxis of reconciliation.

Epilogue

Sitting in the assembly at St. Agatha Church on Chicago's west side, you cannot miss the large newsprint sheet proclaiming the unfolding vision of the people of St. Agatha. Hanging there since October 2007, bearing the signatures of over 120 parishioner families, it has become a bit frayed, but no one wants it taken down or replaced.

As you leave the church, a framed copy of the vision meets your eye. Visitors, always receiving a warm welcome, will often be pointed to this by a parishioner whom they have asked about the parish.

In our bulletin/worship aid each week, the vision greets the eyes of those who have just read the pastor's weekly reflection.

Over the last two years our six vision teams, or Dream teams as we call them, have been working toward that vision. There have been ebbs and flows to the ideas and energy put into the specific goals and objectives that have emerged from our planning process and our twice-a-year convening of the Dream teams to assess our faithfulness, our progress, and adjustments in next steps. The process of gathering in these biannual meetings always creates a revitalized energy.

Our parish pastoral council and parish finance council have incorporated the foundational principle of Appreciative Inquiry that moves us away from focusing on problems and instead focuses us on new possibilities. The groups call each other on this when we move into problem solving mode rather than possibility building/enhancing.

Frustrating the realization of the vision, however, are the lack of necessary resources to achieve our goals. Often it is more about the resource of time than money. We are in an economically depressed area, so creativity about how to accomplish things without money tends to flourish. Time is a valuable commodity, especially when working with many single parents and families where both parents work at least one or two jobs.

Also frustrating our moving forward has been the death of three key leaders from the parish from cancer, ALS, and a heart attack. Although a great loss to our community, one of our members reminded our Dream team that we should not look on their deaths as a "problem." Instead, we recognized that they now are in a special place where they can help us as we call forth new leaders. As part of the communion of saints that we believe in as Catholics, they now lead us in a different way, not spiritually absent, but creating a physical absence in which to call forth new leaders. This has compelled me on a regular basis to invite our parishioners to call forth leaders, or to step forward themselves, to be trained to take on leadership roles. Some have done so; others need added encouragement.

Building a breadth and depth of leadership is now one of the key components in building our vision. This was not an area of focus that was part of the original goals and objectives emerging from the vision, but has naturally presented itself because of the deaths of those key leaders. Therefore, one of our current vision projects is to raise enough funds for fifteen to twenty parishioner/leaders involved in liturgy, marriage ministry, young adult ministry, and youth ministry to annually attend the Archbishop James P. Lyke Conference held specifically for ministers in the black community. Education and spiritual formation of leaders in each of the Dream teams has been an essential element of working toward the realization of the vision.

The one great benefit of the process has been a real sense of empowerment embraced by parishioners at St. Agatha. There has always been a deep commitment to faith and family in the parish. There has also been a great resilience in this community that has suffered the deleterious effects of systemic and spatial racism, as well as the pain of betrayal by the prior pastor who abused a number of youth from the parish and community. The Appreciative Inquiry process has helped people reclaim some sense of control over their future as a parish community and a pilgrim people "Walking in Faith and Moving Forward with Christ." It has helped them move on, still attentive to the safety of children, still hurt at times by occasional reminders of past betrayals, yet having a greater sense of being united in purpose. They know that their gifts will be welcomed and utilized for the good of the vision created out of deep trust in a faithful God, great respect for one another, and unflinching hope in what we can continue to become with the help of God.

In my meetings with other pastors and occasionally with parishioners from other parishes, I encourage them to engage in a visioning process. Most parishes have a mission; few have a stated vision. Since going through this process, I cannot help but believe that the Appreciative Inquiry model could have an incredible impact on other faith communities and, perhaps if engaged at the diocesan level, on the culture of the greater church.

Rev. Larry Dowling
Pastor
St. Agatha Catholic Church

The DNA of Appreciative Inquiry

5 Key Principles

1. The Constructionist Principle: we create our own reality.

2. The Principle of Simultaneity: change doesn't happen as the last step in a process, but happens throughout the process.

3. Poetic Principle: the organization is an open book—we can choose our focus.

4. The Anticipatory Principle: we create what we expect.

5. The Positive Principle: a positive image leads to positive action.

5 Generic Processes[1]

1. Choose the positive as the focus of inquiry;

2. Inquire into stories of life-giving forces;

3. Locate themes that appear in the stories and select topics for further inquiry;

4. Create shared images for a preferred future; and

5. Find innovative ways to create that future.

---

[1] Jane Magruder Watkins and Bernard J. Mohr, *Appreciative Inquiry: Change at the Speed of Imagination* (San Francisco: Jossey-Bass/Pfeiffer, A Wiley Company, 2001), 37.

Appreciative Inquiry 4-D Cycle

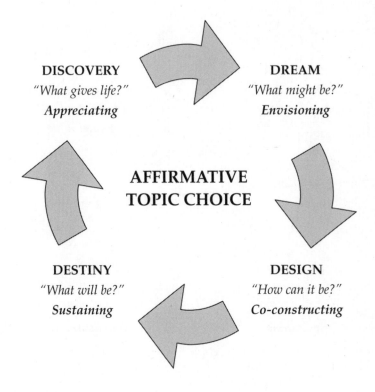

DISCOVERY
"What gives life?"
Appreciating

DREAM
"What might be?"
Envisioning

**AFFIRMATIVE
TOPIC CHOICE**

DESTINY
"What will be?"
Sustaining

DESIGN
"How can it be?"
Co-constructing

David L. Cooperrider and others, *Appreciative Inquiry Handbook: The First in a Series of AI Workbooks for Leaders of Change* (Brunswick, OH: Crown Custom Publishing, Inc., 2005), 5.

Appreciative Discernment 4-D Cycle

DISCOVERY

How does God bless us?

Appreciating

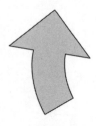

DREAM

What is possible with the grace of God?

Envisioning

AFFIRMATIVE TOPIC CHOICE

DESTINY

What will I do for us to be faithful?

Sustaining

DESIGN

What does us being faithful look like?

Co-constructing

Adaptation of Appendix B.

St. Agatha Parish
Leadership Meeting: Outline

What is Appreciative Inquiry and can it help St. Agatha move forward?

I. Context setting

II. AI theory and principles

Appreciative Inquiry (AI) is a theory of organizational dynamics that holds that an organization will move toward that about which it most persistently inquires. So to bring about change/reconciliation, you don't focus on the problem or the conflict. You don't ask: What's the problem and how do we fix it? Instead, AI theory suggests that you must inquire about that which gives you life and your dreams for the future and then design a way to live into that vision. While the theory comes from the secular social sciences, it is applicable to church use because it recognizes the uniqueness of every organization and the application of the theory is "home grown."

AI is based on 5 key principles. They are:

1. The Constructionist Principle: we create our own reality.

2. The Principle of Simultaneity: change doesn't happen as the last step in a process, but happens throughout the process.

3. Poetic Principle: the organization is an open book—we can choose our focus.

4. The Anticipatory Principle: we create what we expect.

5. The Positive Principle: a positive image leads to positive action.

III. Interview process

IV. AI process

The 4-D cycle

Appreciative Discernment: Four Ds for a Church

> **Discovery:** How has God blessed us and been faithful to us? Where has grace been present? (leads to living in gratitude)

> **Dream:** Who does God call us to be? What awesome future is possible with the grace of God?

> **Design:** What does our being faithful look like?

> **Destiny:** This is our/my commitment to being faithful!

V. Can Appreciative Inquiry help St. Agatha to move forward?

Key success factors

1. Belief that God is ever faithful and that St. Agatha has been powerfully blessed and has the promise of a faithful future.

2. Commitment of parish leadership to the process
   - positive participation and vocal advocacy for the process

3. Hardworking core team
   Core team:
   - Fr. Larry and myself
   - 8-12 people who are a cross section of the parish (drawn from this group?)
   - able and willing to invest the time
     - 2 meetings: approximately 6 hours to map out the process (Definition phase)
     - meeting after each phase of the process to review the results and to continue the tasks of process leadership

4. The bigger the investment the bigger the reward
   - Get everyone to participate!
   - What is the time commitment?

St. Agatha Leadership Meeting: Interview Guide

July 17, 2007

Name of one being interviewed: _____

Name of one doing the interview: _____

Topic: We're faithful, prayerful, and serving an awesome God.

Questions:

1. How long have you been a member of St. Agatha, and please tell me a little about the areas/activities of the parish where you have been active?

2. When you think back over your time as a parishioner, can you recall a story where you were really proud of being a member of the parish? Maybe it is a story of a "peak experience"? Maybe it is a story of a time when you were most engaged and excited about the parish?

3. Without being modest, name three traits that you most *value about yourself* and that you bring with you to St. Agatha.

   1)

   2)

   3)

4. When you think about St. Agatha, what are the factors that are *essential* to who we are, those *attributes* that, if they were absent, we would cease to be a parish that inspires our pride?

5. Imagine for a moment that changes in your life situation dictate that you move to a new city and that you have to leave the parish. Five years from now, you return to the city and you rejoin St. Agatha. You are amazed to see the wonderful ways in which the parish has grown in faithfulness. *What is it that you see and are amazed by?*

6. Imagine that one day you are praying and God speaks to you and commends you for what a fine parish you are a part of. And God promises to grant any *three prayers that you have for the parish*—what do you pray for?

Discovery Phase Interview Guide

St. Agatha Catholic Church is
Walking in Faith and Moving Forward with Christ

**Session One—How has God blessed us? Discovering what
gives us life!**

September 16

*For over one hundred years, St. Agatha Catholic Church has walked
in faith. Through joys and sorrows, through the ups and the downs,
faith has carried us this far. In Jesus we have known a brother who
brings us into intimate union with his Father in heaven, a union that
makes us all one as brothers and sisters in God's family.*

*With courage and conviction we are ready to move forward with
Christ and we begin by remembering and celebrating the many ways
that God has been present and faithful to us. God has always been
faithful to us and has blessed us. Together, we continue to walk our
journey with Christ.*

*We want to discover the revelation of God that has been a part of
our past and present and to use those life-giving blessings as the foundation for dreaming a vision of a faithful future. We discover that
revelation in the stories of our lives. Please give witness to the wonders
that you have seen.*

Name of interviewer (your name): _____

Name of person you interviewed: _____

I. Establishing a comfortable safe place to dialogue

   1. How did you come to join this church? What was it that
      attracted you to join? Who were some of the first people that

you met? Who helped you to feel welcomed? What were some of the activities that you first became involved in?

2. Can you tell me a little bit about your participation in the parish today?

II. Discovering the positive core

1. As a parish, obviously, we have had our share of ups and downs. The very fact that you are here is a powerful witness of your continuing commitment to St. Agatha. What are the memories that you draw on to sustain your continued involvement? Do you have a favorite memory of your participation here at St. Agatha? Please tell me a "highlight" story of being a part of this parish?

2. Coming together in prayer is part of the life of our church. *We are a vibrant and Spirit-filled church.* Can you tell a story and share a favorite memory of a time when a worship service, a day of prayer, or a sermon really touched you? Please share a story about a time when you really felt like the Holy Spirit was present and working in the church? Can you give witness to how the Holy Spirit is present in your life?

3. We want to celebrate the perseverance and courage that we have shown as a parish and we want to build upon that past. *We are one: united and strengthened in Christ.* Can you share a story of a time when you most felt united to others in the parish? When did being a parishioner here feel like "family" to you? What was the event? Who were the people that were a part of that event? How did you help create that sense of family/community?

4. Every Sunday we end Mass by committing ourselves to "*be church after church.*" We all know that being faithful is more than a Sunday morning activity; faithfulness is something that we live all week, individually and as a parish. Can you please share an example with me of how you personally try to live the commitment to be church after church?

5. When you think about the neighborhood that surrounds St. Agatha, how do you see the role of St. Agatha? What is the most positive contribution that St. Agatha makes to the neighborhood community? What does that service look like? How is St. Agatha as a parish *Being Church after Church*?

6. We know that as a church we have received many blessings from God that have made us who we are—blessings that are at the core of who we are as a parish. As we continue our journey with Christ, we want to build upon that positive core. As we move forward, what qualities, traits, or characteristics do you see in the parish that we need to be sure to carry into the future?

7. We believe that God blesses St. Agatha through the gifts that God gives each of our parishioners. Now, this is a hard question, but without being modest, think about yourself for a moment and tell me a bit about the gifts that God has given to you that you bring with you to St. Agatha? Can you share with me three gifts or blessings that you bring to St Agatha?

III. Engaging the imagination and uncovering the dream

1. Through all of our ups and downs, God has blessed us and has been with us. We trust that God will continue to bless us, to work miracles in the life of each of us and in the life of the parish. I want you to imagine that you have moved away from the city for a while, but then you move back to the city and you join St. Agatha Catholic Church again. Use your imagination, be creative and courageous, and describe to me the new St. Agatha that you see. What has the parish become? What miracles has God worked here? What do you see when you look at St. Agatha in 2015?

   • What does our worship look and feel like?

   • How are we relating to one another as a community?

- What is the "imprint" that St. Agatha has left on the neighborhood, the city, the world? What has become the legacy of St. Agatha during the years that you were gone?

2. Imagine that you and God are having a conversation and God promises you that he will answer any three prayers that you make for St. Agatha. What would your three prayers be?

Thank you for sharing your stories with me; I'm grateful to have heard them and that I have gotten to know you better! We are going to share these stories as a parish and together decide what dreams and visions we are going to make the reality for St. Agatha's future.

Is there any last thought that you would like to share with me about your hopes and dreams for the future of our church?

Note: This interview guide was reproduced with space available after each question for note taking.

Interview Summary Sheet

St. Agatha Catholic Church is
Walking in Faith and Moving Forward with Christ

[Please fill this out immediately after completing the interview.]

Name of interviewer (your name): _____

Name of person you interviewed: _____

What was the most quotable quote that came out of the interview?

What was the most compelling or exciting story that came out of the interview?

For each of our three topics, identify the most prevalent theme that you heard and summarize it in a couple of words.

1. **Vibrant and Spirit-Filled Church** [sec. 2, question 2]

2. **We Are One: United and Strengthened in Christ** [sec. 2, question 3]

3. **Be Church after Church** [sec. 2, question 4 and 5]

Overall, what is your sense of what is most important to this individual?

Was there an idea or dream that engaged your own imagination and dreaming?

What was the most life-giving moment in the interview for you?

Outline for Session One: Discovery

St. Agatha Catholic Church is
Walking in Faith and Moving Forward with Christ

Session One: Discovery (3.5–4 hours)
September 16

How has God blessed us?
Discovering what gives life to St. Agatha Catholic Church!

I. Welcome and prayer (Fr. Larry, 30 min.)
- A liturgy of the word with lots of singing
- Luke 24:13-34—Emmaus story
- Homily: Pastor's personal reflection
- Service moves into the session without ending (we will conclude the prayer at the end of the session)

II. Introduction to AI and the process specifics (Fr. Bill, 15–30 min.)

III. Mutual Interviews in pairs (2 hours)
- Introduction and Instructions (Fr. Bill, 15 min.)
- First interview (45 min.)
- Break (15 min.)
- Second interview (45 min.)

IV. Small-group formation (30–45 min.)
- Form Dream teams (will be work group for next session)

V. Closing prayer
- Gathering song and prayer
- Lord's Prayer
- Blessing
- Dismissal and song

Session One:
Small-Group Leaders' Guide

St. Agatha Catholic Church is
Walking in Faith and Moving Forward with Christ

Session One: How has God blessed us? Discovering what gives us life!
September 16

Fr. Bill will have formed the groups and told the participants the process that we are going to do; your role is to lead the process.

1. Gather your group and sit together in a circle.

2. Identify yourself as the designated group leader and a member of the core team.

3. Pass out the prayer sheet and briefly describe the ritual of blessing—then lead the prayer.

4. Remind the participants that they are being asked to introduce their interview partner, using the first two questions from the interview guide. Set an example by being the first to introduce your interview partner. Then proceed randomly until everyone has been introduced.

5. When everyone has been introduced, let the group know (remind them) that you will be working together as a group next week. Choose a name for the group and pass around the roster and ask them for contact information. Let them know that you will contact them later in the week to encourage them to come again next Sunday.

6. Make sure that everyone has completed their interview summary sheet and collect them.

7. Also collect the interview guides and let them know that they will be used next week and that you will bring them back to them.

8. Collect the prayer sheets to use next week.

9. Remind everyone to hold this process in prayer and to dream big dreams!

After the closing prayer, the small-group leaders will meet briefly (5 minutes). You will need to copy the roster so that you can turn one copy in and keep a copy to make the phone calls later in the week. Turn in the interview summary sheets. Keep the interview guides and bring them with you to the core team meeting on Tuesday.

Prayer to Consecrate Sacred Space

Gracious and ever-present God, we claim this time and place for you. We dedicate this time, as a time for truth. We dedicate this place, as a sacred place where we will encounter you in our shared stories and dreams. May your Holy Spirit be our companion and guide on our pilgrims' journey of faith.

We sign ourselves now:

✝ Truth be on my mind as I strive to be open to the other's story.

✝ Truth be on my lips that I may speak the truth of my own experience.

✝ Truth be on my ears that I may hear the truth of my brother and sister.

✝ Truth be on my heart that what I hear may rest upon my heart.

AMEN!

Source: Joseph Nassal, CPPS, used with permission.

St. Agatha's Positive Core

St. Agatha Catholic Church is
Walking in Faith and Moving Forward with Christ

Some common themes emerged. These themes point to how this church has been blessed by God. They represent the *Positive Core* on which to construct a future.

1. Welcoming spirit

2. Church is a family

3. Personal invitation to others

4. Good leadership/pastoring

5. Good preaching

6. Spirit-filled people/church

7. Openness to change

8. Desire for new facilities

9. Service ministries and justice ministries

10. Outreach to the neighborhood

11. Perseverance

12. Commitment

13. People are involved

14. We want to grow in number

15. Seriousness about faith

16. A community/village that raises our children

17. Stewardship

18. Care for our children

19. Desire for youth involvement

20. Disciples that help each other

Session Two:
Small-Group Leader's Guide

St. Agatha Catholic Church is
Walking in Faith and Moving Forward with Christ

Session Two: Dream (4 hours)
September 24

Goal: Dreaming: What awesome future is possible with the grace of God! Discerning the invitation and call of God.

1. Gather your group into a circle. Fr. Bill will combine groups for the *human knot exercise.*

2. Return to your individual group. Quickly go around the room and share names. *Explain and lead the Prayer to Consecrate Sacred Space.*

3. *Sharing and developing the dreams that we discovered last week (an hour?)*

    • Distribute the interview guides.

    • Each person is invited to share the dream that they heard in the interview. Then invite the person whose dream it is to add details, expand on the dream; offer specifics. You and the group need to ask questions to help the person engage their imagination and flesh out their dream. Questions like: What does coming to church and Mass feel like? Who all is here? How are people treating each other—what do you see—can you give us an example? What is the most awesome ministry that we are doing? [These are questions that tie back to the three topics.] The goal is to spur their imagination and the imagination of the group.

- Go around the room until all the dreams have been shared and expanded upon. If someone's interviewer is not there, invite the person to tell their own dream and work with that. If people aren't there, but we have a dream that was written up on the interview guide, read those and invite people to comment.
- Engage the group in a discussion with: We have heard many individual dreams, and we want to now be creative and dream together.
  - ○ Of the dream stories that you heard, what most engaged your imagination and gets you excited about our future?
  - ○ What are some of the key elements that we would want to be sure to include in our communal dream? *List these on a flip chart.*

Take a break

4. *Creating the shared dream statement (an hour?)*
   Goal: to put into a narrative the key elements of the communal dream

   - Come back as a group; review the key elements of the communal statement that you listed. Share the guidelines for dream statements (below).
   - *Work together to write the statement. Statement needs to be written in paragraph form, not just bullet points. Write it up neatly on newsprint to be shared.* (A paragraph is enough; keep in mind the three topics.)
   - Don't force your way to consensus; a minority opinion can be the most exciting path and the one that we will decide to take; try to find a way to include it. Solicit everyone's involvement.

Guideline for dream statements

i. *It is desired.* Do we really want it to be the reality?

ii. *It is bold and provocative.* Is it a "stretch" that will attract others?

iii. *State in the affirmative as if it were already the reality.*

iv. *It is grounded.* Are there examples that illustrate that your dream is a real possibility?

5. *Prepare a creative way to present your dream to the whole group (30 minutes).* Try to involve everyone. Presentations of 3–5 minutes only.

Examples:

- It is 2015 and you are St. Agatha's representative accepting an award for the Parish of the Year in the archdiocese. Give us your team's acceptance speech and brag a little about who and what St. Agatha has become.

- St. Agatha has been included in the book: "Best Practices in Catholic Ministry." Why did we get the award?

- Show us what "vibrant and Spirit-filled" looks like in 2015.

- Show us a magazine article titled: St. Agatha—Best Parish in Chicago.

- Act out: "One day in the life of St Agatha—2015."

- Draw a picture of your dream.

- Etcetera, etcetera, etcetera.

Be creative! Don't be afraid to be silly! Be playful!

We continue in the large group.

Outline for Session Two: Dream

St. Agatha Catholic Church is
Walking in Faith and Moving Forward with Christ

Session Two: Dream (4 hours)
September 24

Goal: Dreaming: What awesome future is possible with the grace of God! Discerning the invitation and call of God.

  I. Mass

 II. Lunch

III. Welcome and Prayer (Fr. Larry, 15 min.)

IV. Introduction (Fr. Bill, 15 min.)
- Recap of the discovery session
    - Themes that seem to be emerging (Gifts from God will be posted)

- Describe the task for today—overview
    - The power of positive images
    - Internal dialogue
        - Internal dialogue as a church
    - **Daring to Dream**
        - Build on the positive core—gifts from God
        - Aim higher—then higher. Use some dream quotes.

 ◆ Have a four-year-old's trust that "all things are possible with God." (Censor that adult voice that whispers: That will never happen.)

V. Go to the dream groups; set up circles (2.5 hours)

1. Human knot exercise (two groups together)

2. Directions for the process that the small groups will use.

3. *Sharing and developing the dreams that were discovered last week.* Small group leaders follow the process in the guide.

VI. Dream Presentations (45 minutes)

1. Each group does their presentations and then has a representative read the dream statement.

VIII. Closing prayer and dismissal (Fr. Larry, 5 minutes)

The Dream of St. Agatha
Catholic Church

St. Agatha Parish is a vibrant, faith-filled, family-centered Catholic Christian community. It stands out in the Archdiocese of Chicago as an increasingly diverse, evangelizing community: a place of welcome and outreach to all who hunger for a spiritual home. It is an anchor of hope responding to all who are in spiritual, emotional, and physical need, and a center for social justice that transforms our neighborhood and city. Our soul-stirring African American–centered liturgies with inspiring and motivating preaching and dynamic adult, teen, and children's Gospel choirs draw us into a deeper relationship with Christ, which inspires our commitment to be church after church. Empowering, visionary leadership affords all parishioners a chance to develop to their fullest potential as Christians and share their time and talent. Our church-wide embrace of tithing makes us self-sufficient, enabling us to help other parishes both locally and internationally. Our Campus for Christ features a new worship space that accommodates our 800+ families (and growing!) and a state-of-the-art educational facility for more than 900 children. It incorporates our expanded SAFE program and our adult education and faith formation programs for adults and youth. Our men's membership has doubled and continues to grow. Together with the women of St. Agatha, our men give active witness as evangelizers and mentors to our youth. Our *SAFE Youth Corps for Christ*, over 300 strong, continues to draw area youth into active participation in liturgy while they serve as peer mentors to other youth and as partners with our senior members in our *Wisdom Is Ageless* ministry.

Six Possibility Propositions

1. St. Agatha has doubled in size by being an evangelizing community of vibrant and inviting faith. As a community of inspired, empowered, prepared, and active witnesses to our Catholic faith, we have become the fastest growing Catholic church in the archdiocese. Our success is grounded in our focused efforts to reach out to and invite men, youth, and the inactive/former members of St. Agatha and the other cluster parishes, which are a welcomed blessing and an essential part of St. Agatha.

2. St. Agatha rejoices in our tradition and identity as a vibrant and Spirit-filled Catholic church. Our worship is rooted in the sacraments of our church and a blessed African American Catholic tradition. It is a celebration of the Word of God proclaimed and preached with conviction and song that is inspiring and fills our congregation with a passion to be faithful disciples of Christ.

3. St. Agatha is a church that knows how to be church after church. We have embraced a missionary identity as disciples of Christ and joyfully serve our brothers and sisters. Inspired by the call of justice, we respond with service ministries that are transforming the community of North Lawndale (and beyond).

4. St. Agatha is a community that is united and strengthened in Christ. Our faith is sustained by our shared commitment to one another and we are truly a family of brothers and sisters in Christ. Our many parish programs and activities

sustain and strengthen that bond in Christ. With effective leadership that empowers and recognizes the gifts of all, we are a church with universal active participation. As a family of faith we are united in our ministry of caring for our children and youth as we welcome and foster their participation in the life of the community.

5. St. Agatha is a church that is financially stable and independent. Through our commitment to stewardship and tithing, aided by effective fund-raising, we are building a campus for Christ that is an anchor of hope in our community and a symbol of the renaissance in North Lawndale.

6. St. Agatha Catholic Academy is the anchor institution in the archdiocesan education ministry on the Westside. The academy is an integrated and essential element of our parish and it is with pride that we promote its continued growth and provide facilities and resources that support their drive for excellence.

Outline for Session Three: Design and Doing It

St. Agatha Catholic Church is
Walking in Faith and Moving Forward with Christ

Session Three: Design and Doing It (3 hours)
October 7, 2007

Goal: Designing the future: What is the road that we will walk with Christ? Discerning the invitation and call from God and making a personal and communal commitment to respond in faith.

I. Mass

II. Lunch

III. Welcome and Prayer (Fr. Larry, 15 min.)
   - Present the dream

IV. Design process
   1. Tell the Building a Cathedral story
      - The dream is the destination, but faithfulness is found in the journey; faithfulness is found in the steps that we take; today we start taking the steps.
      - Do what is possible today, and new possibilities emerge tomorrow; tomorrow we take another step in faith and we move forward with Christ.

2. Explain the Open Space process
   - Bringing together passion and responsibility
   - Go to the group that interests you and with which you are willing to do some work; it is OK to leave one group and to move to another. If one group gets done early, then move into another group and keep working, help stimulate ideas that will help make that possibility a reality.
   - Time to be practical: What do you have the authority to decide and what are you willing to take the responsibility for to make happen?
     a. e.g., Not: Fr. Larry and the parish council should start an evangelization program. But: I will commit myself to being a part of our evangelization effort and I'm willing to serve on a planning committee to make that happen. Or: I'm willing to contact the Archdiocesan Office of Evangelization and arrange for someone to come out and talk with us about starting a program, and I'll contact them this coming week.
     b. e.g., Not: St. Agatha Academy will have the best teachers in the city. But: I will volunteer to be an after-school tutor.
   - Think: I will do "what" by "when"
   - Incorporate the good things that are already a part of the parish. We build on the blessings that we have already received. Faithfulness is not something new for us.

3. Read the possibility propositions. (By the core team members who will lead that design effort.)

4. Form the groups; circle chairs; post the possibility proposition; follow the process guide.

V. Reporting to the group

VI. Closing ritual (Fr. Larry)

      • Expression of gratitude and commitment (personal and communal) to walk in faith and to move forward with Christ

Possibility Proposition:
Be Church after Church

St. Agatha is a church that knows how to be church after church.
We have embraced a missionary identity as disciples of Christ
and joyfully serve our brothers and sisters. Inspired by the call
of justice, we respond with service ministries and social action
that are transforming our neighborhood and city.

Design elements/questions?

1. Where do we hear the *"call of justice"* and how will we respond as *"missionary disciples"*?
2. What spiritual, emotional, and physical needs do our brothers and sisters have, and how will we respond with *service*?
3. What *social action* will be a part of our parish ministry?
4. How will we *"transform North Lawndale (and beyond)"*?
5. Other design elements/questions?

Process:

1. Identify yourselves as the facilitator and reporter
2. Lead the Prayer to Consecrate Sacred Space
3. Post and review the possibility proposition
4. Review the task and guidelines
   - Be practical: what do you have the authority to decide and what are you willing to take the responsibility to make happen?
   - Not a time to make recommendations that "Someone should . . ." Rather it is to say, "This is what I can do to make this possibility a reality."

4. Introduce the first design element/question
   - First ask: How are we already doing this well? Where do you already see this being done here?
   - Brainstorm and discuss ideas that will move this possibility toward reality.
     - use newsprint sheet; include *"by whom" and "by when" information*

5. When you have exhausted that discussion; move to the next element/question and repeat.

6. After completing the design, prepare a report for your group to give that tells us how our group is going to "move forward with Christ." *Be specific*.

7. The facilitator and the reporter will need to write up the report and bring it to the follow-up core team meeting on Oct. 9.

Action Plan:
Be Church after Church

Possibility Proposition: *Being Church after Church*

Dream Idea	Activity	Person Responsible	Completion Date	Progress Toward Dream
Increase Employment Opportunities	Develop Resources for a job readiness program	[each activity had a person assigned but are left blank here to honor confidentiality]	January 31, 2008	Outline of activities and resources/ volunteers needed prepared by 11/4/07
	Create Job Bureau of available jobs in trades/ service industry, etc.		January 31, 2008	Outline of activities and resources/ volunteers needed prepared by 11/4/07
Jail Ministry	Offender and ex-offender outreach and linkage to programs		March 31, 2008	Outline of activities and resources/ volunteers needed prepared by 11/4/07
Social Service Resource Network	Develop resource directory of multi-needs programs offered in the area		March 31, 2008	Outline of activities and resources/ volunteers needed prepared by 11/4/07
Social Justice Action Network	Create social justice teams to respond to broader social justice advocacy efforts		March 31, 2008	Outline of activities and resources/ volunteers needed prepared by 11/4/07

Dream Idea	Activity	Person Responsible	Completion Date	Progress Toward Dream
Energy Assistance	Ceda Program at St. Agatha's		November 30, 2007	Outline of activities and resources/ volunteers needed prepared by 11/4/07
Provide Community Service Activities for Youth	Develop monthly service guide to be distributed to area high schools		January 31, 2008	Outline of activities and resources/ volunteers needed prepared by 11/4/07
Create a Safer Community	Return Caps Meetings to St. Agatha		November 10, 2007	Outline of activities and resources/ volunteers needed prepared by 11/4/07
Expand Ministers of Care	Provide English-speaking Minister of Care to Mt. Sinai on Sundays		November 30, 2007	Outline of activities and resources/ volunteers needed prepared by 11/4/07
Community Beautification	Block gardens on vacant land— city attention to blvd.?		Spring 2008	Outline of activities and resources/ volunteers needed prepared by 11/4/07

Notes

Introduction, pages ix–xv

[1] Peter Steinfels, *A People Adrift: The Crisis of the Roman Catholic Church in America* (New York: Simon & Schuster, 2003), 3.

[2] James D. Ludema, "From Deficit Discourse to Vocabularies of Hope: The Power of Appreciation," in *Appreciative Inquiry: An Emerging Direction for Organizational Development*, ed. D. L. Cooperrider and others (Champaign, IL: Stipes Publishing L.L.C., 2000), chap. 29.

Chapter One, pages 3–15

[1] John Allen, "A Spirituality of Dialogue for Catholics," *Origins* 34 (July 15, 2004): 123.

[2] Dennis Doyle, *Communion Ecclesiology* (Maryknoll, NY: Orbis Books, 2000), 171.

[3] Ibid., 1.

[4] J.-M. R. Tillard, *Church of Churches: The Ecclesiology of Communion*, trans. R. C. De Peaux (Collegeville, MN: Liturgical Press, 1992), 36.

[5] Doyle, *Communion Ecclesiology*, 9.

[6] Ibid., 13.

[7] Henri de Lubac, *The Splendour of the Church*, trans. Michael Mason (New York: Sheed and Ward, 1956), 174–75.

[8] Doyle, *Communion Ecclesiology*, 14.

[9] Ibid., 15.

[10] Ibid., 64.

[11] Henri de Lubac, *Catholicism*, trans. Lancelot C. Sheppard (New York: Sheed and Ward, 1958), 29.

[12] Doyle, *Communion Ecclesiology*, 176.

[13] Ibid., 68.

[14] Ibid., 177.

[15] Ibid., 16.

[16] Ibid., 65.

[17] John Paul II, Apostolic Letter, *Novo Millennio Ineunte* (January 6, 2001): 43.

[18] Ibid.

[19] Ibid.

[20] Ibid.

[21] Allen, "Spirituality of Dialogue," 125.

[22] Ibid.

[23] Ibid.

[24] Ibid.

[25] Ibid., 126.

[26] John Paul II, *Novo Millennio Ineunte*, 56.

[27] Ibid.

[28] Tillard, *Church of Churches*, 48.

[29] Ibid., 48.

Chapter Two, pages 16–39

[1] While I arrived at these considerations independently, it can be noted that they are quite similar to the thought found in John Paul Lederach, *The Journey Towards Reconciliation* (Scottsdale, PA: Herald Press, 1999), chapter 11.

[2] Robert J. Schreiter, "The Distinctive Characteristics of Christian Reconciliation," an unpublished paper made available by the author, 1.

[3] Each of these italicized headings are the same as used by Schreiter in "Distinctive Characteristics." It can be noted that the listing of five elements differs slightly from his earlier work found in *Reconciliation: Mission and Ministry in a Changing Social Order*, although the theological thought is consistent.

[4] Schreiter, "Distinctive Characteristics," 4.

[5] Ibid.

[6] Ibid.

[7] Ibid., 15.

[8] Robert J. Schreiter, *The Ministry of Reconciliation: Spirituality and Strategies* (Maryknoll, NY: Orbis Books, 1998), 19.

[9] Robert J. Schreiter, *Reconciliation: Mission and Ministry in a Changing Social Order* (Maryknoll, NY: Orbis Books, 1992), 34.

[10] Schreiter, "Distinctive Characteristics," 8.

[11] Ibid.

[12] Schreiter, *Ministry of Reconciliation*, 18.

[13] Schreiter, "Distinctive Characteristics," 9.

[14] Ibid., 10.

[15] Ibid.

[16] Schreiter, *Ministry of Reconciliation*, 84.

[17] Ibid., 87.

[18] Ibid., 88.

[19] Ibid., 90–91.

[20] Ibid., 94.

[21] Ibid., 94–95.

[22] Ibid., 95.

[23] Ibid.

[24] Ibid., 95–96.

[25] Ibid., 96.

[26] The source for a complete account of this framework is found in John Paul Lederach, *Building Peace: Sustainable Reconciliation in Divided Societies* (Washington, DC: United States Institute of Peace, 1997).

[27] It can be noted that this progression mirrors the chronological development of Lederach's writings.

[28] Lederach, *Building Peace*, 23.

[29] Ibid., 26.

[30] The use of the web image is found primarily in his later work on conflict transformation.

[31] Ibid., 26.

[32] Ibid., 26–27.

[33] Ibid., 29.

[34] Ibid., 28.

[35] The full text of "The Meeting" and the history of its inspiration can be found in John Paul Lederach, *The Journey Towards Reconciliation* (Scottsdale, PA: Herald Press, 1999), chapter 4. The image is also utilized in an exercise included in Caritas Internationalis, *Building Peace: A Caritas Training Manual* (Vatican City: Caritas Internationalis, 2002). The training exercise is used as part of a process to help participants identify how conflicts sometimes arise out of the emphasis placed on different values. It is this resource that I have frequently modified and used in my own ministry.

[36] Lederach, *Building Peace*, 34–35.

[37] John Paul Lederach, *The Little Book of Conflict Transformation* (Intercourse, PA: Good Books, 2003), 4–5.

[38] Ibid., 14.

[39] Ibid., 9.

[40] Ibid., 31.

[41] Ibid., 10–11.

[42] Ibid., 38. The specific application of this broad framework is beyond the scope of this paper, but can be found in the text cited.

[43] Ibid., 21.

[44] John Paul Lederach, *The Moral Imagination: The Art and Soul of Building Peace* (New York: Oxford University Press, 2005), ix.

[45] Ibid.

[46] Ibid.

[47] Lederach, *Journey Towards Reconciliation*, 99–104.

[48] Ibid., 104–9.

[49] Ibid., 119.

[50] Ibid., 121.

[51] Ibid., 123–36.

[52] Each of these italicized headings is the same as used by Lederach in *Journey Towards Reconciliation*.

[53] Ibid., 125.

[54] Ibid., 128.

[55] Ibid., 130.

[56] Ibid., 132.

[57] Ibid., 135.

[58] See especially *Journey Towards Reconciliation*, part 3: The Call to Reconciliation.

[59] See here Lederach, *Building Peace*. In that work his concern is large-scale global conflict, and, as such, it is less applicable to my own pastoral concern.

Chapter Three, pages 40–62

[1] This quote was also used in a similar way by Jane Magruder Watkins and Bernard J. Mohr in the preface, *Appreciative Inquiry: Change at the Speed of Imagination* (San Francisco: Jossey-Bass/Pfeiffer, A Wiley Company, 2001), xxx.

[2] Ibid., 4.

[3] Ibid.

[4] Margaret Wheatley, *Leadership and the New Science: Learning about Organization from an Orderly Universe* (San Francisco: Berrett-Koehler Publishers, 1994), 8.

[5] Watkins and Mohr, *Appreciative Inquiry*, 6.

[6] Ibid., 7.

[7] Ibid., 9.

[8] Ibid.

[9] Ibid., 10.

[10] Ibid., 14.

[11] The co-constructing principle will be explained in more detail in the next section.

[12] Watkins and Mohr, *Appreciative Inquiry*, 36–40.

[13] David L. Cooperrider and others, *Appreciative Inquiry Handbook: The First in a Series of AI Workbooks for Leaders of Change* (Brunswick, OH: Crown Custom Publishing, Inc., 2005), 13.

[14] Watkins and Mohr, *Appreciative Inquiry*, 37.

[15] This will be illustrated below in the section on the anticipatory principle.

[16] Cooperrider and others, *AI Handbook*, 8.

[17] David Cooperrider and Diana Whitney, "Appreciative Inquiry: A Positive Revolution in Change" (2007), 15. This paper is available in draft form at: http://appreciativeinquiry.case.edu/uploads/whatisai.pdf.

[18] Ibid.

[19] Cooperrider and others, *AI Handbook*, 8–9.

[20] Cooperrider and Whitney, "Positive Revolution," 16.

[21] Cooperrider and others, *AI Handbook*, 9. More about the power of the "inner dialogue" of the organization to shape the future is found below.

[22] Cooperrider and Whitney, "Positive Revolution," 17.

[23] Ibid., 4.

[24] Cooperrider, David L. "Positive Image, Positive Action: The Affirmative Basis for Organizing," in *Appreciative Management and Leadership: The Power of Positive Thought and Actions in Organizations*, ed. S. Srivastva and D. L. Cooperrider (San Francisco: Jossey-Bass, 1990), 91–125.

[25] Cooperrider and others, *AI Handbook*, 10.

[26] Ibid.

[27] Ibid., 11.

[28] Ibid.

[29] Ibid., 12.

[30] Watkins and Mohr, *Appreciative Inquiry*, 39.

[31] Cooperrider and others, *AI Handbook*, 30.

[32] Ibid., 29.

[33] Watkins and Mohr, *Appreciative Inquiry*, 54.

[34] Cooperrider and others, *AI Handbook*, 32.

[35] Ibid.

[36] Ibid., 37.

[37] A more complete description of the 4-D cycle can be found in the *AI Handbook*, chapters 4–7.

[38] Cooperrider and others, *AI Handbook*, 38.

[39] Ibid., 39.

[40] Ibid., 86.

[41] Other methods for doing the interviews are possible.

[42] Cooperrider and others, *AI Handbook*, 87–99.

[43] Ibid., 39.

[44] Ibid., 112–16.

[45] Ibid., 40.

[46] Ibid., 143.

[47] Ibid., 142.

[48] Ibid., 41.

[49] Ibid., 41, 176.

[50] Watkins and Mohr, *Appreciative Inquiry*, 45.

[51] Cooperrider and others, *AI Handbook*, 181. For a more complete account of appreciative organizing competencies see: Frank Barrett, "Creating Appreciative Learning Cultures," *Organizational Dynamics* 24, no. 1 (1995): 36–45.

[52] Watkins and Mohr, *Appreciative Inquiry*, 25.

[53] A list of various forms of engagement of Appreciative Inquiry can be found in James Ludema and others, *The Appreciative Inquiry Summit: A Practitioner's Guide for Leading Large-Group Change* (San Francisco: Berrett-Koehler Publishers, Inc., 2003), 12. This book is an invaluable resource for understanding the AI summit process and offers very practical guidance for one leading such a process.

[54] Watkins and Mohr, *Appreciative Inquiry*, 195.

[55] Ibid., 197.

[56] Ibid., 123–26.

[57] Ibid., 198.

Chapter Four, pages 65–83

[1] The Charter for the Protection of Children and Young People came out of the United States Catholic Conference of Bishops' meeting in Dallas, 2005. It has been widely distributed and is available at http://www.usccb.org/ocyp/charter.shtml.

[2] Margaret Ramirez, "New Pastor Aims to Heal Wounded Congregation," *Chicago Tribune*, February 22, 2007, News Section.

[3] It is a Roman Catholic Church practice to count the total number of worshipers at all the Masses celebrated during the month of October.

[4] Mayna A. Brachear, "Charged Pastor's Principal Fired," *Chicago Tribune*, June 8, 2007, News Section.

[5] Azam Ahmed, "Priest Admits to Abuse," *Chicago Tribune*, July 3, 2007, Metro Section.

[6] David L. Cooperrider and others, *Appreciative Inquiry Handbook: The First in a Series of AI Workbooks for Leaders of Change* (Brunswick, OH: Crown Publishing, Inc., 2005), 52–53.

[7] See appendix D for the outline used for this session.

[8] Margaret Ramirez, "New Pastor Aims to Heal Wounded Congregation," *Chicago Tribune*, February 22, 2007, News Section.

[9] Cooperrider and others, *AI Handbook*, 37.

[10] This refers to question 4 on the interview guide we used. See appendix E.

[11] The call list used was a Fall 2006 list of registered and active parishioners.

[12] Jane Magruder Watkins and Bernard J. Mohr, *Appreciative Inquiry: Change at the Speed of Imagination* (San Francisco: Jossey-Bass/Pfeiffer, 2001), 91.

[13] Further information on the defining of the interview protocol and the crafting of good questions can be found in Cooperrider and others, *AI Handbook*, 88–92, and Watkins and Mohr, *Appreciative Inquiry*, 91–93.

Chapter Five, pages 84–96

[1] James Ludema and others, *The Appreciative Inquiry Summit: A Practitioner's Guide for Leading Large Group Change* (San Francisco: Berrett-Koehler Publishers, Inc., 2003), 121–23.

[2] See appendix H for an outline of the session. This outline was not distributed but was used by the core team.

[3] James Ludema and others, *The Appreciative Inquiry Summit*, 128–29.

⁴ See appendix I for the instructions that the small-group leaders followed.

⁵ Jane Magruder Watkins and Bernard J. Mohr, *Appreciative Inquiry: Change at the Speed of Imagination* (San Francisco: Jossey-Bass/Pfeiffer, A Wiley Company, 2001), 56.

Chapter Six, pages 97–108

¹ The outline for this session is found in appendix M.

² This quotation was found at: http://www3.thinkexist.com/quotes/Daniel_H._Burnham/.

³ The inspiration for this process was the consensus visioning exercise in James D. Ludema and others, *The Appreciative Inquiry Summit: A Practitioner's Guide for Leading Large-Group Change* (San Francisco: Berrett-Kohler Publishers, Inc., 2003), 152–59.

⁴ In the literature this is the criteria used for provocative propositions, but I have found it equally useful as dream or vision criteria.

⁵ Ludema and others, *The Appreciative Inquiry Summit*, 158.

⁶ Ibid, 159.

Chapter Seven, pages 109–18

¹ One team member was uncomfortable with the use of "provocative proposition" in a church setting. While I like the phrase and do not think it inappropriate, there was no reason to make an issue of it, and we adopted the alternative phrase, possibility proposition. See appendix O for the possibility propositions that were developed.

² Jane Magruder Watkins and Bernard J. Mohr, *Appreciative Inquiry: Change at the Speed of Imagination* (San Francisco: Jossey-Bass/Pfeiffer, A Wiley Company, 2001), 153–54.

³ This method is described in detail in Harrison Owen, *Open Space Technology: A Users Guide*, 2nd ed. (San Francisco: Berrett-Kohler Publishers, Inc., 1997).

⁴ This process will be described more fully in the next section.

⁵ See appendix P for the outline for this session.

⁶ Owen, *Open Space Technology*, 98.

⁷ The small-group leader's guide for one of the possibility propositions can be found in appendix Q. Similar guides were prepared for each of the six design groups working on the individual possibility propositions.

[8] See appendix R for one such report. Similar actions plans were developed for each of the six possibility propositions.

Chapter Eight, pages 121–28

[1] I did not make an audio recording of this discussion but took detailed notes. The comments reported are paraphrased replies unless they are set off in quotation marks, which are direct quotes taken from my notes. To protect anonymity, usually I will not attribute the comment to a specific core team member.

[2] The current St. Agatha Church is a consolidation of four parishes. As part of an Archdiocese of Chicago pastoral planning process, in 2004 ten Westside parishes were consolidated into four parishes. Blessed Sacrament Church, Our Lady of Lourdes, Presentation Church, which had previously been in a cluster with St. Agatha, were now closed and they became a part of St. Agatha. I was aware that there were still "unfinished" effects of that merger because in one of the initial meetings that I had with the St. Agatha parish leadership team, this core team member said that for her the need for reconciliation at St. Agatha was not the effects of Daniel McCormack's actions. Rather, her sense of a need for reconciliation was that the parishioners from the closed parishes were not yet equal members of St. Agatha. This was her feeling, even though she was on the parish council and was widely involved in the life of the parish. At the time, my response to her was that the Appreciative Inquiry process did not require that we identify and analyze the problems; rather, the focus was going to be on the positive core of the parish and the dreams for the future. For that reason, I said the value of AI is that all issues and sources of conflict will get addressed, but will get addressed from the side of the "solution."

[3] The question of timing is an important praxis consideration and will be addressed more fully later.

[4] E-mail message to the author, October 17, 2007.

Chapter Nine, pages 129–42

[1] This quote was first used in chapter 2 as part of an explanation of the philosophical underpinnings of Appreciative Inquiry.

[2] See particularly Susan Star Paddock, *Appreciative Inquiry in the Catholic Church* (Plano, TX: Thin Book Publishing, 2003); and Mark Lau

Branson, *Memories, Hopes, and Conversations: Appreciative Inquiry and Congregational Change* (Herndon, VA: Alban Institute, 2004).

[3] See p. 5 for a review of these elements. The exception is that that there is no expressed concern for *ressourcement*. I do not think that this is in any way a criticism of the parish, but in the individual dream narratives and in the common dream developed through the process, no one made reference to the New Testament communities, such as described in Acts 2:42-47. I have no explanation for this and I do not think that it was detrimental to the process or the results. Nor do I think that it detracts from my observation that St. Agatha is an expression of communion ecclesiology.

[4] Desmond Tutu tells the story of the peace process in South Africa in his book, *No Peace Without Forgiveness* (New York: Doubleday, 1999).

[5] J.-M. R. Tillard, *Church of Churches: The Ecclesiology of Communion*, trans. R. C. De Peaux (Collegeville, MN: Liturgical Press, 1992), 48.

Conclusion, pages 143–52

[1] The definitive resource on this method is found in Kay Pranis and others, *Peacemaking Circles: From Crime to Community* (St. Paul, MN: Living Justice Press, 2003).

[2] A simple description of Appreciative Discernment is found on pp. 68–70 or in appendix C. In my research I have not found any other use of the phrase.

Bibliography

Allen, John. "Journalism and Polarities in the Church." *New Theology Review* 19, no. 3 (August 2006): 24–32.

————. "A Spirituality of Dialogue." *Origins* 32 (July, 15, 2004): 122–26.

Branson, Mark Lau. *Memories, Hopes and Conversations: Appreciative Inquiry and Congregational Change*. Herndon, VA: Alban Institute, 2004.

Caritas Internationalis. *Building Peace: A Caritas Training Manual*. Vatican City: Caritas Internationalis, 2002.

Cooperrider, David L. "Positive Image, Positive Action: The Affirmative Basis for Organizing." In *Appreciative Management and Leadership: The Power of Positive Thought and Actions in Organizations*, edited by S. Srivastva and D. L. Cooperrider, 91–125. San Francisco: Jossey-Bass, 1990.

Cooperrider, David L., and others. *Appreciative Inquiry Handbook: The First in a Series of AI Workbooks for Leaders of Change*. Brunswick, OH: Crown Custom Publishing, Inc., 2005.

Cooperrider, David L., and Diana Whitney. "Appreciative Inquiry: A Positive Revolution in Change." A draft form of this paper is available at: http://appreciativeinquiry.case.edu/uploads/whatisai.pdf.

De Lubac, Henri. *Catholicism*. Translated by Lancelot C. Sheppard. New York: Sheed and Ward, 1958 [French orig. 1938].

————. *The Splendour of the Church*. Translated by Michael Mason. New York: Sheed and Ward, 1956 [French orig. 1953].

Doyle, Dennis M. *Communion Ecclesiology*. Maryknoll, NY: Orbis Books, 2000.

John Paul II. Apostolic Letter, *Novo Millennio Ineunte* (January 6, 2001). The document can be found at: http://www.vatican.va/holy_father/ john_paul_ii/apost_letters/documents/hf_jp-ii_apl_20010106_ novo-millennio-ineunte_en.html.

Lederach, John Paul. *Building Peace: Sustainable Reconciliation in Divided Societies*. Washington, DC: United States Institute of Peace, 1997.

———. *The Journey Towards Reconciliation*. Scottsdale, PA: Herald Press, 1999.

———. *The Little Book of Conflict Transformation*. Intercourse, PA: Good Books, 2003.

———. *The Moral Imagination: The Art and Soul of Building Peace*. New York: Oxford University Press, 2005.

———. *Preparing for Peace: Conflict Transformation Across Cultures*. Syracuse, NY: Syracuse University Press, 1995.

Ludema, James D. "From Deficit Discourse to Vocabularies of Hope: The Power of Appreciation." In *Appreciative Inquiry: Rethinking Human Organization Towards a Positive Theory of Change*, edited by D. L. Cooperrider and others, 265–87. Champaign, IL: Stipes Publishing L.L.C., 2000.

Ludema, James D., and others. *The Appreciative Inquiry Summit: A Practitioner's Guide for Leading Large-Group Change*. San Francisco: Berrett-Kohler Publishers, Inc., 2003.

Owen, Harrison. *Open Space Technology: A Users Guide*. 2nd ed. San Francisco: Berrett-Kohler Publishers, Inc., 1997.

Paddock, Susan Star. *Appreciative Inquiry in the Catholic Church*. Plano, TX: Thin Books Publishing, 2003.

Schreiter, Robert J. "The Distinctive Characteristics of Christian Reconciliation." Unpublished paper made available by the author, photocopied.

———. "The Ministry of Forgiveness in a Praxis of Reconciliation." Lima, Peru: International Seminar on Reconciliation, August 21, 2006, photocopied.

————. *The Ministry of Reconciliation: Spirituality and Strategies*. Mary-knoll, NY: Orbis Books, 1998.

————. *Reconciliation: Mission and Ministry in a Changing Social Order*. Maryknoll, NY: Orbis Books, 1992.

Steinfels, Peter. *A People Adrift: The Crisis of the Roman Catholic Church in America*. New York: Simon & Schuster, 2003.

Tillard, Jean-Marie. *Church of Churches: An Ecclesiology of Communion*. Translated by R. C. De Peaux. Collegeville, MN: Liturgical Press, 1992 [French orig. 1987].

Tutu, Desmond. *No Future Without Forgiveness*. New York: Doubleday, 1999.

Watkins, Jane Magruder, and Bernard J. Mohr. *Appreciative Inquiry: Change at the Speed of Imagination*. San Francisco: Jossey-Bass/Pfeiffer, A Wiley Company, 2001.

Wheatley, Margaret. *Leadership and the New Science: Learning about Organization from an Orderly Universe*. San Francisco: Berrett-Koehler Publishers, 1994.

Index

4-D cycle (model), 51, 53–57, 60

5-D cycle (model), 57, 89

accompaniment, 25, 27, 38, 137, 148

Allen, John, 3, 13–14

analogical imagination, 9, 15

analogies, 9–10, 15

Appreciative Discernment, 68–75, 89, 92, 150–51, 158

Appreciative Inquiry (AI)
definition, 42
DNA of, 43, 156
anticipatory principle, 46, 48, 156
constructionist principle, 43, 156
five generic processes, 50–51
poetic principle, 46, 156
positive principle, 47–48, 82, 156
principle of simultaneity, 44, 67
process, 42, 44–46, 48, 50–61, 67–69, 71–74, 86–87, 98, 101, 106, 111, 115, 121–24, 126–37, 141–42, 145–51, 155

Appreciative Inquiry Handbook (Cooperrider and others), 72

Appreciative Inquiry Summit: A Practitioner's Guide for Leading Large-Group Change (Ludema and others), 86, 104

Avon, Mexico, 59, 61

Building Peace: Sustainable Reconciliation in Divided Societies (Lederach), 38

Catholic Common Ground Initiative, 3, 13

Catholic Theological Union (Chicago), 19

church
as Body of Christ, xi, 7–9, 12, 152
as leaven, 9
as pilgrim people of God, 8–9, 155

communion
horizontal and vertical dimension, 8, 11, 26, 130, 135

Communion Ecclesiology (Doyle), 4

communion ecclesiology, 3–5, 10–12, 130, 134–35, 146
    five dimensions, 6–12
conflict, 12, 19–20, 22, 28–29, 61, 138–41, 144–45, 147, 149
    as the focus of process, 38, 140
    as opportunity, 29–31, 37
    epicenter and episode, 30–31, 37
    within church, ix–xi, xiv, 32–36, 152
conflict transformation, 27–28, 30–31, 33, 37
Cooperrider, David L., 40, 45, 48, 51, 76
core team, 54, 68, 72, 74–77, 80–81, 83–88, 93–99, 102, 104–17, 121–28, 132–34, 136–37, 147–49
Definition phase, 57, 71, 74, 83, 148
de Lubac, Henri, 6–7, 10
Design phase, 55–56, 110
Design teams, 56, 115
Destiny/Doing It phase, 56–57, 109
dialogue, 3–4, 12–15, 26, 31, 141, 144, 146
    in AI process, 44, 49–50, 52–55, 57, 59, 61, 75, 95, 103, 133, 137–38, 140, 150
discernment, 34, 69, 87–88, 101
Discovery phase, 53–55, 69, 115
Dowling, Larry, xiii, 65–68, 71, 73, 87–89, 95, 98–99, 106, 112, 116, 125, 127–28, 155
Doyle, Dennis M., 3–5, 7, 9, 134–35
dream narrative (*see also* vision statement), 100–103, 107, 135

Dream phase, 54–55, 95, 105
dream presentations, 103–5
Dream teams, 55, 94, 97, 100, 153–54

Eucharist, 5, 7–9, 11–12, 134–35
    as a sacrament of reconciliation, 12, 151

facilitation, 68, 88–90, 137
forgiveness, 17, 20, 33, 24, 138
"From Deficit Discourse to Vocabularies of Hope: The Power of Appreciation" (Ludema), xii

hospitality, 11, 25–26, 137, 148
human knot exercise, 97, 100, 102, 106

imagination, 44–46, 78, 82, 85–86, 103, 111, 140–41
Incarnation, 17
inner dialogue, 49–50, 78, 99, 136, 149
interview guide, 53–54, 73, 81–83, 90–95

John Paul II, Pope, 10–11, 14, 132
Journey Toward Reconciliation, The (Lederach), 32

leadership, x–xiii, 49, 53, 55, 60–61, 69–72, 74–75, 80, 88, 95, 98, 110, 127–28, 133–34, 137, 145–48, 151, 154
Leadership and the New Science: Learning about Organization from an Orderly Universe (Wheatley), 41

Lederach, John Paul, 17, 27–39, 130, 133, 139–41, 146, 149
Ludema, James D., xii
Lumen Gentium, 7

Matthew 18, 34–36, 38
McCormack, Daniel, 65, 67, 71, 78, 90, 124–26, 148–49, 200
"The Meeting" (Lederach), 29
Memories, Hopes, and Conversations: Appreciative Inquiry and Congregational Change (Mark Lau Branson), 58
memory, 21–22, 26–27, 29, 38, 45, 49, 112, 133, 136, 148
Mohr, Bernard J., 43, 50, 52, 57, 59, 72, 81, 95, 110, 156
moral imagination, 28, 31–32, 38, 140, 146
Moral Imagination: The Art and Soul of Building Peace (Lederach), 32
mutual interviews, 53, 55, 72–73, 76, 90, 102

narrative (story)
    (*see also* dream narrative)
    containing identity, 20–21, 27, 136
    in AI process, 44, 46–47, 49, 51–54, 61, 73, 79, 82, 90–93, 95–96, 103, 107, 135–36, 140–41, 144, 148
    in ministry of reconciliation, 29, 38, 140, 144–45
    master narrative of reconciliation, 22
    of the lie, 20–22, 27, 136

new sciences, 41–42
Newtonian physics, 40–41
Novo Millennio Ineunte (John Paul II), 10, 14, 132

open space technology, 56, 110–11, 113–14, 116
Owen, Harrison, 110, 114

Peacemaking Circles, 144
People Adrift: The Crisis of the Roman Catholic Church in America, A (Steinfels), ix
Polak, Fred, 50
polarization (in the church), xiv, 3–4, 12, 150
positive affect, 47, 85–86
positive core, 47, 51–52, 54, 56, 91, 98, 110, 128, 130, 140, 145, 150
positive focus, 42, 48, 52, 60, 90, 118, 130
positive image, 48–50, 61, 99, 101–2, 105, 115
"Positive Image, Positive Action: The Affirmative Basis for Organizing" (Cooperrider), 40, 48
praxis
    of communion, 11, 13, 15
    of reconciliation, xi–xii, 20, 24–39, 131, 133, 136–45, 147–52
prayer, 12, 87, 89, 92, 94, 96, 99, 106, 112, 116, 132, 135, 151, 174
Precious Blood Ministry of Reconciliation, xi, xiv–xv, 144
problem solving, 59–60, 125, 140, 154

provocative propositions, 55–57, 109

possibility propositions (statements), 56, 109–11, 113–14, 118

purpose
defining (at St. Agatha), 74–80
statement, 75, 77–78, 88, 130

Pygmalion effect, 49

questions, 44–48, 50, 53, 57, 69, 82, 91–93
crafting of, 45–46, 54, 82
foundational questions (in AI), 52, 73, 82

reconciliation
as a locus, 26, 29
communities of, 26–27, 38
concerned with relationships, 21, 28–31, 34, 37, 129–30
goal and process, 50, 130
horizontal and vertical dimensions, 18, 20, 26, 37, 130
ministry of Jesus, 24–26, 137
mission of Jesus, 9, 17–19, 36
new creations, 18, 21, 37, 133, 136, 139, 148–49

Schreiter, Robert J., xiv, 17, 19–27, 36–39, 130–31, 133, 135–41, 144, 148–49

Shumpert, Gregory, 73

spirituality
of communion, 5, 10–12, 132, 151
of dialogue, 12–15, 133
of reconciliation, xiv, 19–24, 27, 36–39, 87, 131, 138

sponsor statement, 87

Srivastva, Suresh, 51

Stavros, Jacqueline M., 76

Steinfels, Peter, ix

storytelling, 53, 82, 90, 96

summit, Appreciative Inquiry (AI), 58, 67, 85, 86, 104, 109

Taylor, Frederick, 41

Tillard, Jean-Marie, 4, 15, 142

topics, 51, 56, 73, 89, 92, 123–24, 129–30
criteria, 53, 76
for faith communities, 79–80
topic selection (choice), 52–53, 74–77, 79, 134

Truth and Reconciliation Commission, 16, 141

truth telling, 27, 35, 38, 61

valuation, 96

vision statement, 101, 103

vulnerable transparency, 34–35

Watkins, Jane Magruder, 43, 50, 52, 57, 59, 72, 81, 95, 110, 156

Wheatley, Margaret, 41

Whitney, Diana, 45, 48, 76

whole system, 28, 80, 82, 106, 110